THE SILVER LINK LIBRARY OF RAILWAY MODELLING

•

LAYOUTS FOR LIMITED SPACES

Best wishes in all your modelling

Nigel Adams

24/1/98

THE SILVER LINK LIBRARY OF RAILWAY MODELLING

●

LAYOUTS FOR LIMITED SPACES

Choice * Design * Construction * Operation

●

Practical solutions for the space-starved modeller

Nigel Adams

Silver Link Publishing Ltd

First published in September 1996

British Library Cataloguing in Publication Data

A catalogue record for this book is available from the
British Library.

ISBN 1 85794 055 5

Silver Link Publishing Ltd
Unit 5
Home Farm Close
Church Street
Wadenhoe
Peterborough PE8 5TE
Tel (01832) 720440
Fax (01832) 720531
e-mail: pete@slinkp-p.demon.co.uk

Printed and bound in Great Britain

Please note that the reference on the cover to Paul Mayes
('Bembridge' layout) should read Paul Mays.

Frontispiece Shops and houses with their back gardens in
Station Street on Charles Insley's Irish-themed Caher Patrick
layout. In all the rich detail, the narrow gauge railway is almost
incidental as it curves away towards the hidden sidings at the
rear of the layout! *Martin Hewitt*

Below Gordon Gravett's Llandydref layout, showing how the
buildings effectively mask the very tight curve to the fiddle
yard - in fact, the line in the foreground passes through the
works and shed to return behind the water tower on the left.
Gordon Gravett

CONTENTS

INTRODUCTION

For as long as I have been modelling - which is over 45 years, including my childhood - I have been attracted to small layouts. When I was in the Oxford MRC I did help to build two large layouts (Radley and Rewley Road), and I have operated them and enjoyed doing so, but when it comes to my own layouts I have never even considered building a large one. Of course, it is true to say that I have not always had the space to allow me to do so, but even when that has been the case, I have not taken the opportunity. That probably says something about me and my outlook on life - perhaps I am one of those who say small is beautiful!

Undoubtedly, one of the attractions of small layouts for me is that they are easy to transport to and from exhibitions and are quickly set up and dismantled, and I like exhibiting. You meet a lot of very friendly people, and it is good to be able to share experiences and ideas with fellow modellers and members of the public who wish to find out more about our hobby. I have found that I learn most by seeing and reading about actual layouts. Presumably I am not alone, as the central feature of *Railway Modeller*, and other magazines, over many years has been the 'Railway of the Month'.

Therefore in the first part of this book I set out my ideas about layouts in limited spaces, while the second part is about layouts that I and other modellers have built in various gauges. I am pleased to say that the other modellers also share some of their thinking about small layouts.

Obviously, a great deal of this book is based on my own experience, but I know that over the years I have consciously or unconsciously adopted other people's ideas and, no doubt, some people may even have adopted mine. To all these people whose ideas I have used, my thanks.

ACKNOWLEDGEMENTS

Many people have helped me with this book and I would particularly like to thank all those who have written about their layouts and provided photographs and plans. Thanks, too, to the photographers who have taken photos either of the layouts or the prototype and have readily agreed that they could be used.

Special thanks are due to Peter Honeybone who has drawn almost all of the plans, sketches and prototype layouts, to Martin Hewitt, who has taken many of the photographs, and to John Raybould who proofread the text for me. Peter, Martin and John are fellow members of COVGOG - the Coventry Gauge O Group - of which I was a founder member. I was also a founder member of the Oxford & District MRC in 1966, and of the Leamington & Warwick MRS in 1974, so I have been involved in model railway groups on and off for nearly 30 years.

I owe a great debt to Sue Temple, who deciphered my handwriting in four exercise books and spent many hours typing the manuscript for me. Without her, this book would not have got off the ground.

Finally, I could not have been a railway modeller for all these years without the active support and encouragement of my family. Celia has always been very supportive of my modelling time, Justin helps to operate layouts at shows and with the electrical side of the layouts, as well as building his own, and Paul now exercises his artistic and graffiti skills when asked.

It is to them that I dedicate this book.

1.
WHY BUILD SMALL LAYOUTS?

Very often people build small layouts as a matter of necessity. Modern houses are usually 'compact' (a euphemism for 'small') compared with older houses of, say, 50 years ago. For three years we lived in a 1930s semi-detached house, which was much bigger than the modern detached house we moved into in 1974 when I moved my job. The 1930s house also had a large loft that would have been great for a layout, whereas modern houses have roof trusses that make putting a layout in the loft a virtual impossibility. So some people are forced into building layouts in limited spaces.

On the other hand, some people - including myself - actually prefer small layouts. In his book *An Approach to Model Railway Layout Design* (subtitled 'Finescale in small spaces'), Iain Rice says that he finds that a relatively small layout has a stronger appeal and that he relates better to it, and I share those sentiments. Maybe it is because I like building and exhibiting layouts; with a small layout, you can build it, exhibit it for a few years then sell it or dismantle it and build another one, learning from what you did on the previous one.

You can also progress with a small layout. I have great admiration for those people who have a master plan for a large layout and build it to completion over a number of years, but I have to say that this is not for me. There is a great risk that I would lose interest because it would not be completed quickly enough. Perhaps I am impatient.

There are also a number of other very pertinent circumstances which favour small layouts. First, there's time. Very few of us have unlimited time for our hobby. Time is a precious commodity and all sorts of things have a prior claim on it - not least earning a living to finance our railway modelling activities! Which leads to the second consideration - cost. A small layout is cheaper. Ready-made track and points are expensive, and the limited space means that you do not need to buy so much trackwork, or scenic materials and rolling-stock. In addition, the small layout will probably use short-wheelbase locos, which are cheaper than the large tender engines or diesels.

Third, our modelling skills, like most things in life, improve with practice and experience, and if we build a large layout over a long period the later modelling tends to be of a higher standard than when we first started, and sometimes it shows. However, if we build a small layout it is easier for the modelling to be of a uniform standard.

Fourth, small layouts are easily portable in case of house moves, etc, which can be a big consideration in these days when people may have to move more frequently than in years gone by. Also, the fact that a layout is easily portable means that it can be exhibited with few problems. It is quite easy to built a layout that will fit into a 'large Mini' (for example a Metro, Corsa or Fiesta) with all the necessary stockboxes, toolbox, etc. Large layouts need a lot of work to dismantle them and a large van and a number of helpers to get them to an exhibition; then time is spent erecting the layout for the show, and dismantling it again at the end, reloading it into the van and re-erecting it at home. For me, at any rate, that is the unacceptable face of railway modelling!

I once had a small layout that easily fitted into the back of a family car. It measured 6 ft 6 in by 1 ft 4 in and was split into two halves for transit. The pieces were bolted together face to face, and the bottom board had castors so that, once out of the car and into the hall, it could be *wheeled* to its position and erected.

I have since seen someone who has taken this a stage further. The castors are simply screwed to a piece of blockboard, the dimensions of which are slightly larger than that of the baseboard sections. Once at the exhibition, the 'trolley' is put on the ground and the crated layout is dropped onto it and wheeled in.

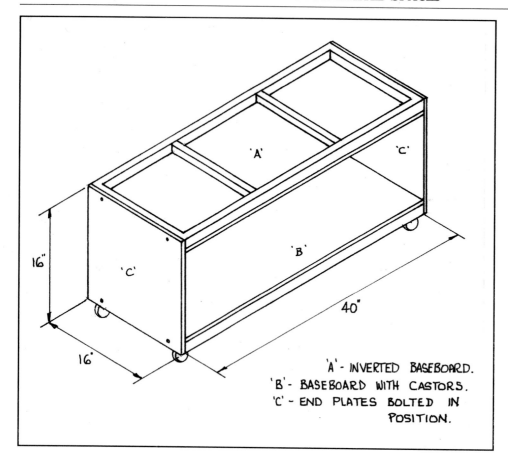

'A' - INVERTED BASEBOARD.
'B' - BASEBOARD WITH CASTORS.
'C' - END PLATES BOLTED IN
             POSITION.

'Crated' baseboards transported face-to-face separated by end plates, and with castors for ease of manoeuvrability.

vicarage was built in 1977, and is what might be called functional. However, it has plenty of storage space. In each of two larger bedrooms there are two large built-in wardrobes. At one time we stored two layouts in one of them, one (OO gauge) measuring 5 ft 6 in by 1 ft 4 in belonging to my elder son (Justin), and one measuring 5 ft 6 in by 1 ft 10 in belonging to me. Both were stored on their end and were simply lifted out of the cupboard and placed on two trestles for working on or operation.

In my study there is another walk-in cupboard under the stairs, which I seriously considered as a site for a small layout but, in the end, decided against it. Another potential site in many houses is the alcove between an end wall and chimney breast; I have seen a very good N gauge layout at exhibitions built to fit in such a space.

A number of people have built layouts on coffee tables; Ray Arnold built such a layout in 3 mm scale some years ago. Other people have built small layouts almost solely for exhibitions. One that springs to mind is Llanastr by Rodney Hall. This was an EM layout measuring 6 feet by 1 ft 3 in, which folded in half horizontally (ie 3 feet by 2 ft 6 in) for transport. He built it when living in a flat and it easily fitted into his car for transport to and from shows. An article about it appeared in *Model Railway Journal* (No 4 in 1985).

In his book *An Approach to Model Railway Layout Design*, Iain Rice says that 'Llanastr was one of the smallest, and certainly one of the most beautifully executed, of finescale layouts to have appeared in recent years' because it 'made use of the brilliantly simple device of employing a sector table not just to provide a fiddle yard, but also to substitute for more than half of the pointwork.' He had one reservation; he felt that the fiddle yard should be hidden to increase the modelling potential. He therefore

Finally, there is no need to assume that small layouts mean small gauges. It depends on the space available and the type of layout you want to build. For example, I have an O gauge layout on a board measuring 3 ft 9 in by 1 ft 10 in!

What is a small layout?

'How small is small?' is the basic question here, and I am sure that there are many definitions of a 'small layout'. The Gauge 0 Guild's definition is one of 16 feet or less in length. Some *very* small layouts have been built. For example, when I was in the Oxford MRC many years ago, a member built an N gauge layout that fitted into a violin case! That was undoubtedly small, but I would call it a 'micro' layout.

Very often, the size of a layout is dictated by circumstances rather than by choice. It may be that the layout cannot be accommodated permanently in any room in your home, so the size is dictated by the available *storage* space rather than the space where the layout is operated. In a way this can be quite liberating, because you can store the compact layout in a cupboard and erect it for working on or operation in any of the main rooms of the house.

To quote a couple of actual examples, my present

designed 'Elan' to fit into a space 6 ft 6 in by 1 ft 9 in and to fold into a 'suitcase-sized box' measuring 3 ft 3 in by 1 ft 9 in.

It can therefore be seen that to answer the question 'What is a small layout?' is virtually impossible, because it depends so much on whether the layout is designed to be accommodated in a specific storage space, to be brought out for working on and operating, or whether it is intended to be permanently erected in a limited display space. In either case the layout would be easily transportable to exhibitions, which as mentioned above is, in my opinion, a bonus. However, to attempt the impossible, here is *my* definition of a small layout: 'A layout that fits into a limited space, either for permanent display or for storage, and which is easily carried by one or two people.'

Types of small layout

There are various types of layout that can be fitted into limited spaces, but it is true to say that some are more suited than others. Apart from in the smaller scales (such as Z, N and OO9) the continuous layout is unlikely to suit small spaces.

The very first small layout that I had experience of operating was Les Eden's 'Bossington Branch', an OO gauge layout of the terminus-to-fiddle-yard variety. Its single baseboard measured 6 feet by 1 ft 6 in, plus a separate fiddle yard, and had the great advantage that all the shunting moves took place within the confines of the main baseboard. To add spice to the operation it was worked to a tape-recorded commentary, which had built-in 'recovery time', during which certain features on the layout were described - but it really *was* a sin if you got yourself into such a mess that you had to stop the tape! Even though it is now over 25 years since I operated the layout, I can still remember that the tape started by saying, 'There really is a place called Bossington. . .'

There are many other terminus-to-fiddle-yard layouts that have appeared at shows and in the model railway press. Some are very compact and some are stored in racks for ease of transport, but the basic idea is well known to modellers.

Sometimes the idea is extended so that the lay-

out is fiddle-yard-to-station-to-fiddle-yard. I built one such layout in 7 mm narrow gauge, based very loosely on Brynglas on the Talyllyn Railway. This was easily transportable, too (see pages 69-72).

Models of loco sheds or works can be suitable for small spaces; indeed, these are particular favourites of mine, and I have built a number over the years, one in 009, two in 7 mm narrow gauge and two in 7 mm standard gauge. One of the 7 mm standard gauge layouts can be operated as a loco shed or a wagon repair works, and is capable of sustaining considerable operator and viewing interest. (Photographs and plans of these layouts appear in Chapter 7.)

A freight yard is another possibility; I think there is far more operating potential on a layout with goods wagons than there is with passenger workings. A variation on this theme is a quarry; there have been a number of such layouts on the exhibition circuit and I particularly remember two. One was an excellent little 009 layout called Bryn Mawr Quarry by Martin Williamson. It was very much a minimum-space layout, measuring only 34 by 18 inches, and was described in the August 1984 issue of *Scale Model Trains*. Despite its size it was packed with scenic features. The same plan could, of course, be used in 0-16.5 by roughly doubling the dimensions to 68 by 36 inches.

The other layout I remember watching for a long time at a Manchester Model Railway Exhibition some years ago was one by Geraint Hughes called Rise End

Geraint Hughes's Middlepeak Wharf incline. Note the use of the incline to mask from the front of the layout (right) the exit to the fiddle yard at ground level. Note also the chains on the incline, the shed with its door open - to permit the modelling of some interior detail - and the dustbin outside the building on the left. *Railway Modeller*

Quarry. The visible section of the layout measured only 8 feet by 1 foot, and it rested on a framework measuring 10 feet by 1 ft 6 in. The framework was larger than the layout to allow for a rear shelf for controls, stock, etc. The layout was based on a branch line on the Cromford & High Peak Railway and had a very effective working stone-loader.

Geraint Hughes has also built another superb layout, again based on the Cromford & High Peak, called Middlepeak Wharf. This was fully described in the June and July 1993 issues of *Railway Modeller*. It is a transit yard and has four exits from the visible part of the layout. It also features a working wagon incline. I have seen it at exhibitions and it is an impressive little layout. Plans and photographs of these three layouts are also shown in Chapter 7.

These are just a few of the possibilities, and I have no doubt there are others. The choice is yours!

Where to put small layouts

There are many places where one can accommodate small layouts. Again, it depends primarily on whether you wish to operate them in situ or store them and erect them elsewhere.

Let us take stored layouts first. I had two layouts stored in the garage, one (The Shed Mark II in O gauge - see page 80) measuring 11 feet by 1 ft 8 in (two boards each 5 ft 6 in long), and the other measuring 3 ft 9 in by 1 ft 10 in, which really is a minimum space layout in O gauge (see page 83). Here you

need protection from the dust, but this is no problem. A polythene sheet covered the larger layout, held in place by bulldog clips, while the smaller layout had a hardboard cover. They stood on trestles for operation. The wiring was all self-contained, so it was simply a matter of plugging in the AC supply and the hand-held controller and the layout was ready to operate.

Another method is to crate the layout and store it in a suitable place. When I was a curate I lived in a semi-detached house and my modelling activities took place in a shed, where my layout, 'Tile Hill', was stored in its carrying frame. This worked very well, as it could be 'unpacked' and operated in the shed, while for exhibitions it was crated and put in the back of the car with the stock, etc.

Earlier I mentioned that I had considered building a layout in a cupboard in my study, and I would not have been the first to build one in an understairs cupboard - Cyril Freezer did so with his Tregunna branch many years ago. Another alternative is to build a storage area in a living room.

About 25 years ago I modelled in 009 and when we moved to a large pre-war semi-detached house in Ramsey Road my father-in-law made a storage cabinet from ½-inch plywood covered in 'Fablon'. The front was hinged to drop down, the layout slid in on runners and the stock and tools, etc, were stored underneath. The unit was of such a height that our eldest son could stand at it and use the top as a playing surface - it was very successful.

A further alternative is to display the layout permanently in the living area, and make it look good. A

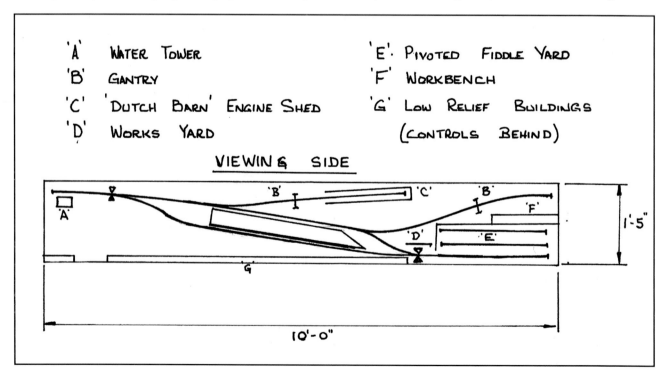

Below left and right A plan of 'Tile Hill' and its carrying frame, a very convenient way of storing a small layout.

number of years ago a modeller named Dave Howsam built a layout above some bookshelves round his living room. The layout was covered in matching material and, from the photographs in *Railway Modeller* at the time, it looked very effective.

A number of modellers have also built layouts around the walls of a main bedroom. John Peverel-Cooper (a founder member of the Oxford MRC) did this. It was also very effective, and we always reckoned that he could sit in bed and operate the layout! His scheme also had the advantage that the space beneath it was neatly covered by curtains hanging at the front and was used for storage.

The design of some houses produces unusual areas for a layout. A friend from Theological College days had a vicarage with a very long and wide landing, ideal for a layout if he had been a model railway enthusiast!

Iain Rice makes the point that, when looking for a site for a layout, we tend only to think in two dimensions - width and length. We forget height. It may be possible to find space for a layout *above* existing furniture. As a vicar I should be attract-

The 'Ramsey Road' storage box with its drop-down front.

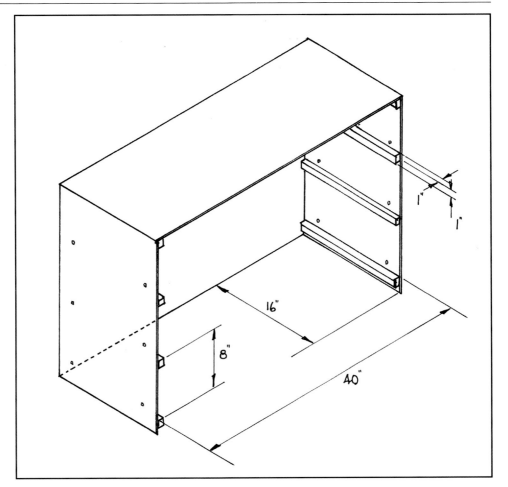

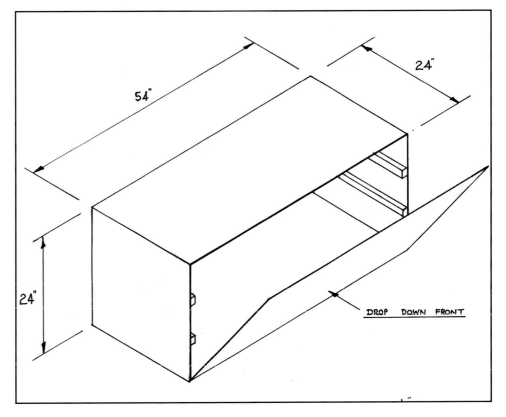

ed by what he calls 'the Vicarage Study' baseboard. The basic board is at such a height as to bridge the desk or bookcase and two extension pieces are folded over the top or added on. As Iain says, the principal advantage of this is that the bulk of the rolling-stock can remain on the layout instead of being packed away and re-railed every time you want to operate the layout.

Twice in my modelling career I have used a garden shed; the first, in 1968, measured 6 feet square, the second, in 1988, was 12 by 8 feet. In both cases the shed was carpeted and lined with polystyrene 1 inch thick, with black polythene between the polystyrene and the outer shed timbers; the polystyrene was cut to the correct size to fit between the inside upright battens. I will be the first to admit that a shed is not the

ideal place for a model railway, but it is certainly quite acceptable. The main safety consideration is the installation of the electricity supply. In both my sheds I ran the cable from the mains supply on a stretcher bar to a main box just inside the shed. An alternative is to bury the cable under the ground. Either way, if in doubt consult a qualified electrician!

Perhaps the best alternative, if it is available, is to take over a suitable spare room. Our sons have grown up and one has left home, so I am lucky to have the use of the smallest bedroom (9 ft 10 in by 7 ft 8 in) as a modelling room. This is the ultimate! The layout is on one side of the room, standing on old kitchen units, and on the other side is an old wardrobe, used for storage, my workbench and a chest of drawers on which stands my toolbox.

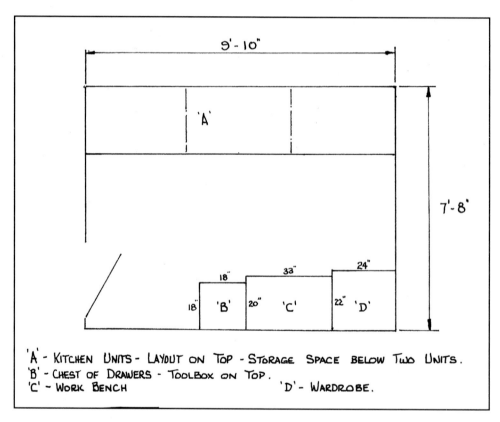

The railway room.

2.
PROTOTYPE IDEAS

People wishing to start a model railway often think that it will be impossible because they cannot fit in all that they want to in the space available. However, there are a number of space savers in the prototype that can easily be incorporated into a model.

Stations

First let us take the simple fiddle-yard-to-terminus layout beloved of so many space-starved modellers. On many such layouts there has to be a run-round loop to enable the loco that has hauled the train in to uncouple and run round, either to depart again or to go to the shed, and there are many such prototypes. Obviously the headshunt and the points take up space, but this need not be the case. We tend to think of single points (left-hand, right-hand or Y, straight or curved). However, if you are prepared to think of three-way points, double slips, etc, there are immediate space savings.

Three prototypes with space-saving elements quickly come to mind. One is the Bembridge branch on the Isle of Wight, an excellent prototype for a layout in a limited space. The branch was 2¾ miles long and ran from Brading through St Helens to Bembridge. It closed in September 1953, but even in its last summer of operation there were 17 trips in each direction on weekdays, 20 on Saturday and 12 on Sunday. The branch operated under the 'one engine in steam' regulation, and the number of coaches was increased from two to three on summer Saturdays to cope with the additional holiday traffic.

The branch began at Brading Junction and the only intermediate station - St Helens - was three-quarters of a mile from Brading. A few yards beyond the station was a ground frame, which gave access to St Helens Quay. This formed part of Bembridge Harbour, which, judging by the size of the large goods

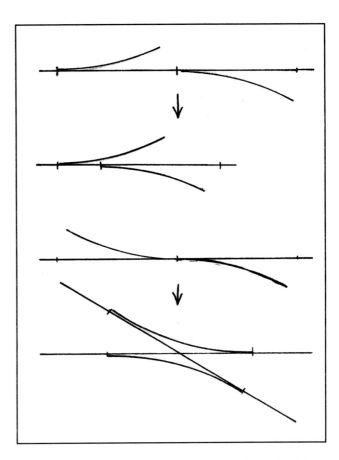

Space saving: two single facing turnouts can be replaced by a three-way point, and a trailing and facing point can become a single or double slip.

shed, the two cranes, etc, never fulfilled the potential envisaged by the promoters in 1874.

The engines ran bunker-first from Brading to Bembridge. When a train arrived at Bembridge, the fireman uncoupled the engine and the driver took it on to the turntable at the very end of the platform road, which was then aligned with the run-round loop. In theory the engine could be fully turned and run round its train to

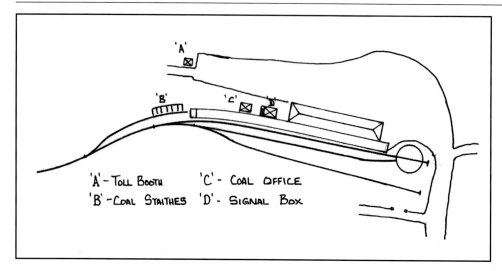

'A' - TOLL BOOTH   'C' - COAL OFFICE
'B' - COAL STAITHES   'D' - SIGNAL BOX

Left Plan of Bembridge station, Isle of Wight.

Below left No 14 *Fishbourne* on the turntable at Bembridge on 24 March 1950. The fireman is aligning the table with the run-round loop, enabling the driver to take the loco round to the other end of the train. *Neil Davenport*

on the merchandise siding and two vans were occasionally stored there too, used by the engineers as a mobile workshop and a tool store.

From a modelling point of view, two or three typical 'O2' Adams 0-4-4 tank engines, four coaches and six or seven open wagons would be plenty of stock and allow for spares and the occasional repair to be done.

Paul Mayes has made a beautiful model of Bembridge on three 40 by 15 inch baseboards, including the traverser (ie 10 feet by 1 ft 3 in). The three boards are stored in a carrying case for ease of storage and transport. The layout was described in the September 1995 issue of *Railway Modeller*, and is also featured in Chapter 7.

Also on the Isle of Wight, Ventnor station was very hemmed in - trains burst out of the tunnel straight into the station. Here is just the prototype for those modellers who do not have much length available and want the departing train to run through a tunnel into the fiddle yard almost immediately after it leaves the station.

Ventnor also gives the lie to the statement I have often heard that a loco shunting a station should not have to keep shunting in and out of a tunnel. Even when the loco was running round the stock it had to enter the tunnel before it could set back. The other interesting feature of Ventnor was that access to the island platform across the track was via a gangplank (like those used to board a ship), which was stored on the platform (see the photograph opposite) and positioned when required.

depart bunker first; in practice it usually just ran round and departed chimney first. As all the locomotives used were small tank engines, this arrangement was a considerable space saver. When the driver drove the engine off to the departure end of the station, the fireman locked the turntable back into position for the platform road, ready for the next arrival. While all this was happening, the guard went to the signal box to operate the points to allow the driver to recouple to the train.

As can be seen from the plan above, the station layout was very simple. The only sidings were one on the north side of the line serving a coal and coke wharf, and a general merchandise siding alongside the run-round loop. There was no goods shed, but a box van was used for that purpose as required. The extra coach used to strengthen the set on summer Saturdays was also stabled

Right Plan of Ventnor station, Isle of Wight.

Below right A view of Ventnor station showing how the line came out of the tunnel straight in to the station throat, and how the site was surrounded by hills. *J. Spencer Gilks*

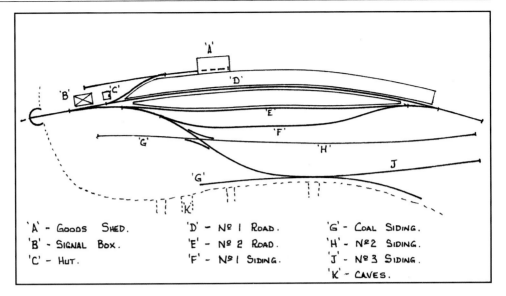

'A' - GOODS SHED.   'D' - Nº 1 ROAD.   'G' - COAL SIDING.
'B' - SIGNAL BOX.   'E' - Nº 2 ROAD.   'H' - Nº2 SIDING.
'C' - HUT.   'F' - Nº 1 SIDING.   'J' - Nº 3 SIDING.
                                                       'K' - CAVES.

Three other prototype possibilities on the Isle of Wight are shown in the plans overleaf - Wroxall, Havenstreet and Cowes - together with one from the Isle of Portland. Islands are often a good source of prototype plans for small layouts. Some years ago Dennis Nix of Amersham MRC built a beautiful model of Cowes.

Birmingham Moor Street station was a terminus with a traverser at the end of the platform road rather than a turntable. Here is a prototype space-saver that was right in the centre of the second largest city in the country.

A non-terminus prototype is provided by Donnington, on the line between Wellington (Shropshire) and Stafford that served Wellington, Hadley, Donnington, Newport Gnosall, Haughton and Stafford. When my late father-in-law photographed it, passenger traffic had been withdrawn, but it was still open for goods traffic. It had distinct modelling possibilities both as a small through station or a goods terminus. The former could be modelled faithfully on the prototype as shown in the plan on page 18. For the terminus the tracks could end at the level-crossing gates, which could be replaced by a low wall, and it would be convenient to add crossovers to facilitate the passenger movements with locomotive run-rounds, as shown on the plan in broken lines.

In either form of station the factory provides a reason for varied goods traffic. In reality it was a general engineering firm, but the modeller could use any special products of his choice, and some interesting loads and workings could be imagined. In addition to the factory, Donnington Army Ordnance Workshops were nearby, which could also provide a reason for more goods traffic and possibly an excuse for introducing some of the range of 4 mm Army tanks and vehicles available in shops and multiple stores.

The passenger traffic could be quite extensive, but that would depend on whether it was modelled as a through station or as a terminus. Whichever was chosen, the following could be accommodated: trains for commuters to Wellington and/or Stafford; trains for workers to and from the factory and the Army workshops; and normal daily branch-line traffic.

There were no motive power facilities at Donnington, but should the modeller wish to add them, it would not be difficult.

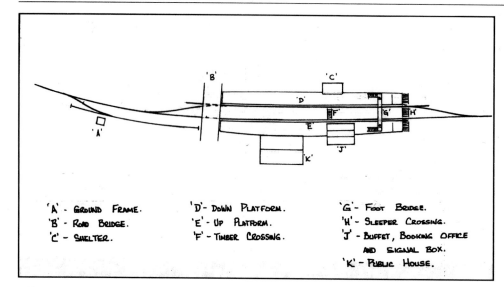

'A' - GROUND FRAME. 'D' - DOWN PLATFORM. 'G' - FOOT BRIDGE.
'B' - ROAD BRIDGE. 'E' - UP PLATFORM. 'H' - SLEEPER CROSSING.
'C' - SHELTER. 'F' - TIMBER CROSSING. 'J' - BUFFET, BOOKING OFFICE
                                               AND SIGNAL BOX.
                                          'K' - PUBLIC HOUSE.

Three more IOW locations providing useful prototypes for small layouts - Wroxall (*top*), Havenstreet (*middle*) and Cowes (*bottom*).

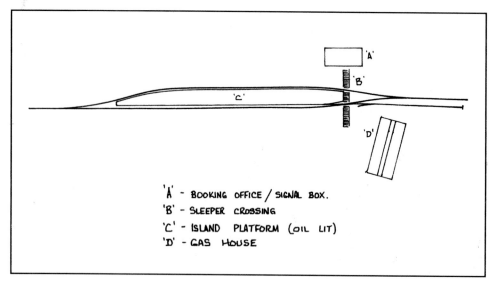

'A' - BOOKING OFFICE / SIGNAL BOX.
'B' - SLEEPER CROSSING
'C' - ISLAND PLATFORM (OIL LIT)
'D' - GAS HOUSE

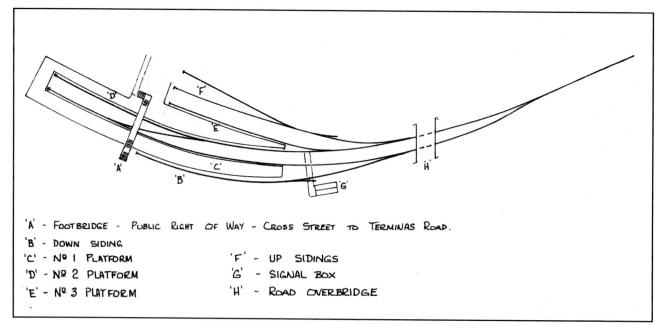

'A' - FOOTBRIDGE - PUBLIC RIGHT OF WAY - CROSS STREET TO TERMINUS ROAD.
'B' - DOWN SIDING
'C' - Nº 1 PLATFORM   'F' - UP SIDINGS
'D' - Nº 2 PLATFORM   'G' - SIGNAL BOX
'E' - Nº 3 PLATFORM   'H' - ROAD OVERBRIDGE

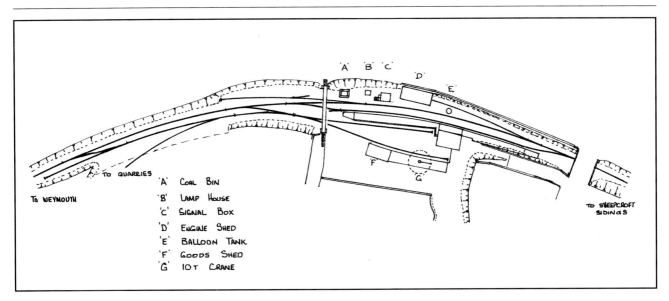

TO QUARRIES

TO WEYMOUTH

'A' COAL BIN
'B' LAMP HOUSE
'C' SIGNAL BOX
'D' ENGINE SHED
'E' BALLOON TANK
'F' GOODS SHED
'G' 10 T CRANE

TO SHEEPCROFT SIDINGS

Above Plan of Easton station on the Isle of Portland.

No 5946 *Marwell Hall* has just arrived at Birmingham Moor Street on 3 September 1960 with the 9.10 am from Kingswear in Devon. The running gear for the traverser and the right-hand wall of the 'pit' are shown in the bottom right-hand corner. *Michael Mensing*

Class '5600' 0-6-2T No 6668 has arrived at Moor Street with a train from Knowle & Dorridge on 28 July 1960; having uncoupled from its train, it has moved over on to the run-round line by means of the traverser. *Michael Mensing*

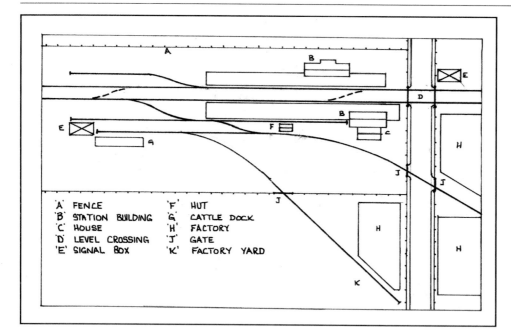

'A' FENCE   'F' HUT
'B' STATION BUILDING   'G' CATTLE DOCK
'C' HOUSE   'H' FACTORY
'D' LEVEL CROSSING   'J' GATE
'E' SIGNAL BOX   'K' FACTORY YARD

Left Plan of Donnington, Shropshire, showing how the layout could be adapted to terminus form.

Below left A view of Donnington in 1967 showing the platforms and the signal box on the other side of the crossing gates. The photograph also shows the bay road, huts and factory buildings beyond. *Harry Bott*

Loco sheds and works

Who says that all layouts must have a station? I am fascinated by loco sheds, and this is quite as advantage if you are like me and have a fair number of locomotives. There is also a further advantage in modelling a loco shed - you don't have to bother about coupling and uncoupling!

Here again the Isle of Wight produces some proto-

type ideas, including Ryde Works, Newport Shed and Ryde Shed. Alternatively there is St Blazey in Cornwall; this was a semi-roundhouse and can be modelled (as Peter Denny has done on his Buckingham Branch) in semi-low-relief.

Another prototype idea is a wagon works, which I think is soaked in railway atmosphere. There is the usual scrap and junk lying around, old wheelsets, etc, and, again, traversers are used.

On the old Somerset & Dorset Railway there was such a repair works at Radstock. (In this particular works some of the buildings would present no modelling problems, as there were no windows!) C. J. Peal wrote a short article about the works in the June 1968 *Model Railway Constructor*. Apparently in 1965 it was one of a number of such works owned by Marcroft Wagons Ltd.

The works carried out general overhauls, and the range of wagons overhauled and repaired there was quite extensive; the last wagon to have been actually built there was a 12T open wagon in 1942. Mr Peal visited the works in October 1965 and saw, amongst others, petrol tank wagons, BR 16-ton minerals, five-plank opens, 13-ton 'Hybar' wagons, three-plank dropsides, a variety of ballast wagons, 20T steel hoppers, 20T coke wagons, and a 'bogie bolster'. As one might expect, a

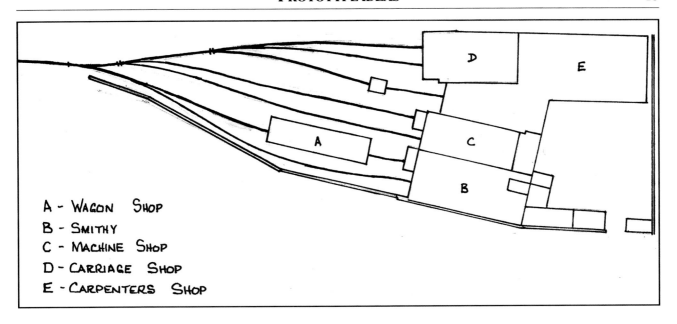

A - WAGON SHOP
B - SMITHY
C - MACHINE SHOP
D - CARRIAGE SHOP
E - CARPENTERS SHOP

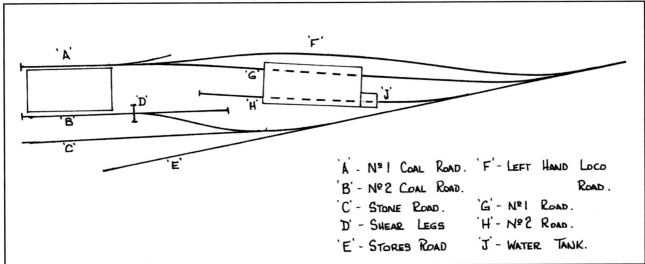

'A' - Nº1 COAL ROAD.   'F' - LEFT HAND LOCO
'B' - Nº2 COAL ROAD.   ROAD.
'C' - STONE ROAD.   'G' - Nº1 ROAD.
'D' - SHEAR LEGS   'H' - Nº2 ROAD.
'E' - STORES ROAD   'J' - WATER TANK.

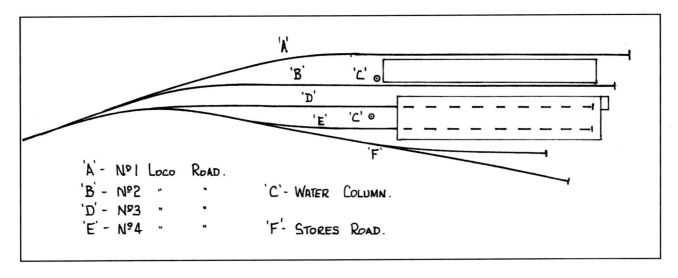

'A' - Nº1 LOCO ROAD.
'B' - Nº2 "   "   'C' - WATER COLUMN.
'D' - Nº3 "   "
'E' - Nº4 "   "   'F' - STORES ROAD.

Three IOW shed/works prototypes - Ryde Works (*top*, as in 1924),
Newport shed (*middle*) and Ryde St Johns Road shed (*bottom*).

Left Ryde St John's Road Shed on 17 July 1958. The detail shown is a small layout modeller's dream! Grass growing up through the ballast, long grass in front of the signal box and growing round the sleeper piles, etc, point rodding, coal/ash piles by the coaling stage, and smoke stains above the entry roads to the shed. *Neil Davenport*

Below Plan of St Blazey shed and its semi-roundhouse.

Bottom Radstock wagon repair works, S&DR.

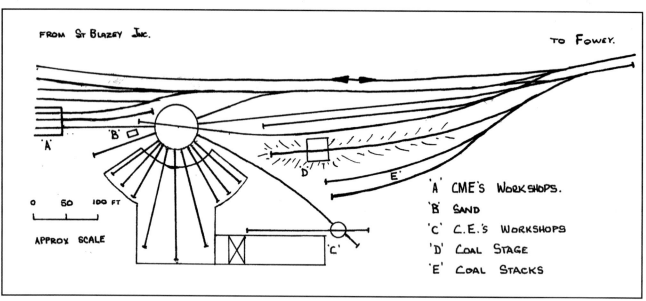

FROM ST BLAZEY JNC.

TO FOWEY.

0   50   100 FT

APPROX SCALE

'A' CME's WORKSHOPS.

'B' SAND

'C' C.E.'s WORKSHOPS

'D' COAL STAGE

'E' COAL STACKS

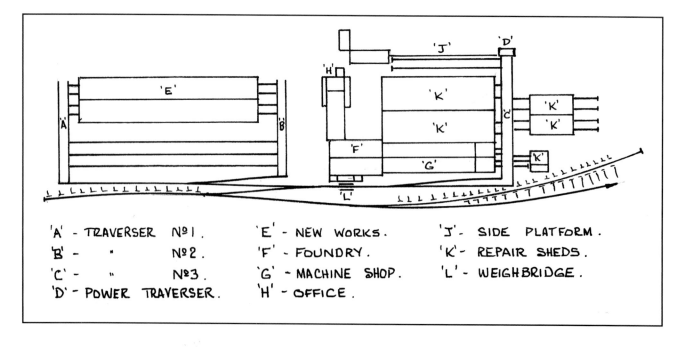

'A' - TRAVERSER Nº1.   'E' - NEW WORKS.   'J' - SIDE PLATFORM.

'B' -   "   Nº2.   'F' - FOUNDRY.   'K' - REPAIR SHEDS.

'C' -   "   Nº3.   'G' - MACHINE SHOP.   'L' - WEIGHBRIDGE.

'D' - POWER TRAVERSER.   'H' - OFFICE.

variety of work was being carried out, with some wagons over pits or on trestles and some jacked up with one set of wheels removed.

The floor of the repair shop was all wood, and the usual paraphernalia of gas bottles, trestles, spare bits and pieces and hand trucks was always to be seen. In the machine shop there were the usual lathes, shapers and slotters for all the machining and turning jobs, as well as drills, guillotines, welding tackle, etc. Painting was performed in the old engine shed at Radstock GWR station, with a nearby grounded van body being used as a paint store.

Wagons arrived and left the works on ordinary service goods trains. Prior to 1964 GWR Pannier and Prairie tank locomotives were used, and after that diesels, which in the late 1960s were 'Hymeks' or 0-6-0 shunters. Within the repair shop, a small shunting tractor moved the wagons around.

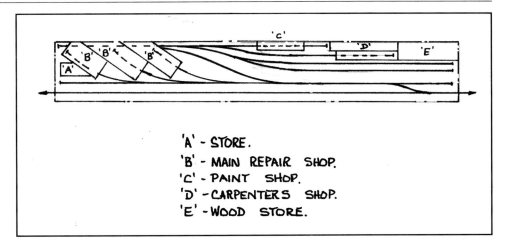

'A' - STORE.
'B' - MAIN REPAIR SHOP.
'C' - PAINT SHOP.
'D' - CARPENTERS SHOP.
'E' - WOOD STORE.

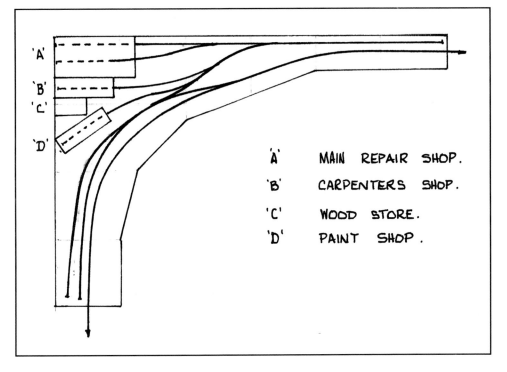

'A'   MAIN REPAIR SHOP.
'B'   CARPENTERS SHOP.
'C'   WOOD STORE.
'D'   PAINT SHOP.

C. J. Peal's two wagon repair works plans based on Radstock.

In his article Mr Peal suggested two possible layout ideas, shown in the accompanying plans. As he wrote his article nearly 30 years ago, I have been unable to contact him, but if he reads this book I gratefully acknowledge my debt to him for the information and plans.

A compact wagon works was described in the *Scale Model Trains* magazine of February 1983. It had no traverser and used standard points, yet still fitted into a space measuring 8 ft 5 in by 2 feet. Ken Rimmell, who built and exhibited it, did so to be able to run and display his collection of private owner wagons. He decided that the only place where one would see a collection of such vehicles from all over the country in pristine condition would be the works where they were built!

Operation consisted of a loco hauling a chassis out

of the erecting shop to the body shop, and the completed wagon then being taken to the hidden siding - ie to its destination somewhere in the UK. The walls of the factory buildings hid the swapping of the chassis for the completed wagon.

Also on the works theme, articles appeared in *Model Railway Constructor* in July and October 1958 describing two possible layouts based on the old depot at New Cross Gate, which served as a repair works and locomotive shed from 1839 to 1947. It was suggested that a corner site could be very effective for housing such a yard.

It was not unusual for even the smallest railway to have its own workshop. For example, the Talyllyn Railway - on which I am a volunteer - has a very com-

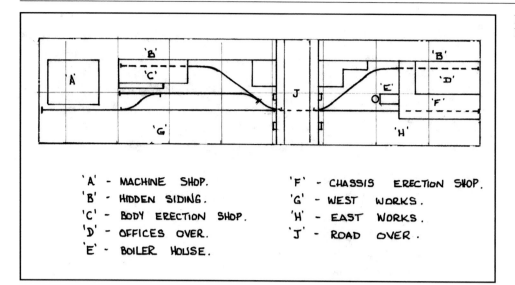

Ken Rimmell's 'O. O. Gage Ltd' wagon works.

'A' - MACHINE SHOP.
'B' - HIDDEN SIDING.
'C' - BODY ERECTION SHOP.
'D' - OFFICES OVER.
'E' - BOILER HOUSE.

'F' - CHASSIS ERECTION SHOP.
'G' - WEST WORKS.
'H' - EAST WORKS.
'J' - ROAD OVER.

A works yard occupying a corner site, based on the New Cross Gate works of the London & Croydon Railway.

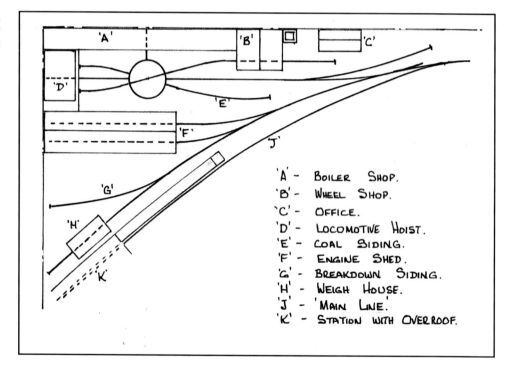

'A' - BOILER SHOP.
'B' - WHEEL SHOP.
'C' - OFFICE.
'D' - LOCOMOTIVE HOIST.
'E' - COAL SIDING.
'F' - ENGINE SHED.
'G' - BREAKDOWN SIDING.
'H' - WEIGH HOUSE.
'J' - 'MAIN LINE.'
'K' - STATION WITH OVERROOF.

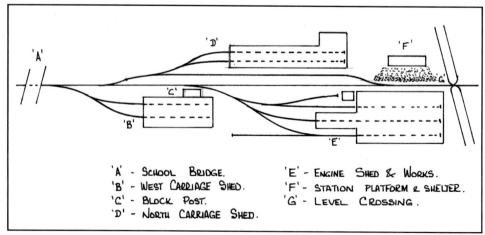

'A' - SCHOOL BRIDGE.
'B' - WEST CARRIAGE SHED.
'C' - BLOCK POST.
'D' - NORTH CARRIAGE SHED.

'E' - ENGINE SHED & WORKS.
'F' - STATION PLATFORM & SHELTER.
'G' - LEVEL CROSSING.

Plan of Pendre Works, Talyllyn Railway.

A general view of the Talyllyn Railway's Pendre yard. Note the sleeper drilling rig outside the shed between th two oil-drums, the stack of spare rails on sleepers, and the wooden walkway in front of the cabless loco on the right. *Author*

pact engine shed and works at Pendre. For someone who wished to model such an installation, it would be very attractive to build the workshop with a removable roof so that all the machinery inside could be shown.

Another idea that I have used twice now, also on works layouts, is a traverser. I built a 7 mm narrow gauge layout and, more recently, a 7 mm standard gauge layout, each of which utilised a traverser to gain access to the engine sheds and other sidings (see pages 65 and 83, Chapter 7). Admittedly, such an arrangement was not common on the prototype, but they were a familiar sight in locomotive works and I think they are acceptable in motive power depots. They are certainly good space-savers.

Another space-saving idea, as with Ventnor station mentioned above, is to gain access to the engine shed via a turntable. There are prototypes for this in a number of places, for example Swanage. I have built two layouts using this method; one was as 009 layout measuring 36 by 20 inches, and the other was a 7 mm narrow gauge layout measuring 5 ft 6 in by 1 ft 10 in (again, see Chapter 7). All of these layouts are, or were, regularly exhibited at shows, and personally I think such layouts are very satisfying to operate. Certainly the traverser or turntable means that there is movement on the layout, which is important - people pay money to see layouts operating.

3.
DESIGNING SMALL LAYOUTS

Portability

The factors that have to be taken into account when designing small layouts have already been touched upon. The first question is whether or not the layout is to be in a permanent location. If it is, all well and good, but if not you will have to decide where and how it is to be stored. This also means that the baseboards will have to be of such a size that they can be easily carried. I accept that some exhibition layouts have baseboards measuring 5 by 3 feet or larger, but that size will have been adopted in the knowledge that a group of people will be available to carry them in and out of the storage area. In the past it has often been said that the maximum size of baseboard that can be easily and safely handled by one person is 4 by 2 feet. From experience I would reduce that to 38 by 20 inches or, if you prefer metric measurements, about 1 by 0.5 metres.

If the layout is to be exhibited, you have to take into account the size of the vehicle in which it will be carried and how it will be carried. Obviously, if you have large baseboards you need a large vehicle; hence the fact that the larger layouts seen at shows require a van to transport them. This usually has to be hired, which is expensive.

Many cars these days are hatchbacks, and these are ideal for transporting layouts. However, they vary in size quite considerably so it pays to take this into account during the early stages of designing a layout. For example, when I worked in the car industry I used to drive a large estate car; it is easy to get a baseboard 5 ft 6 in long into such a vehicle in the load space area, but that is not possible in a Metro, for example, unless you also fold down the front passenger seat; a Metro's load space area with the rear seat fully folded is approximately 40 inches square, which is probably true of a number of vehicles in the 'Supermini' category. Thus if you restrict the length of the baseboard

to 38 inches you can allow for a carrying frame to be constructed in which a number of baseboards can be transported and stored.

While thinking of designing a layout with transport in mind, don't forget that baseboard sections have three dimensions, length, width and height. If the height of the baseboard including scenery is excessive, it will obviously limit how much you can carry in the car. What many people also tend to forget is that you need to carry stock boxes, controllers, lighting pelmets, etc, as well as the layout itself. For example, one of my layouts requires three stock boxes, two plastic stacking boxes, a stool and a lighting pole.

Some people have been very ingenious in the design of their baseboards to allow for the stock to be carried in the baseboard itself. On one of his many exhibition layouts, Ian Futers stored the stock in the fiddle yard board framework, while Peter Gentle on his Minsterley layout stores his stock in drawers within one of the baseboards.

Another way of transporting a layout is to have a folding baseboard; one such design as used on my son Justin's layout worked very well. The only thing to watch is that the scenery on each board is so placed that it does not foul the other when the boards are folded.

Planning

Having dealt with the baseboards, let us now turn to the layout itself. It might be stating the obvious, but unless you have a firm idea of what you are aiming at, it will be very difficult to come up with a convincing design. Iain Rice suggests that what I might call a 'layout specification' should be drawn up before any detailed design work is started. As with any specification, it is almost certainly going to be amended as the design and construction progress, but at least there is a clear specification from which to deviate. I have fol-

An example of a stock storage system.

lowed this practice on a number of my own designs.

As far as the track layout is concerned, it must be designed bearing in mind the stock that is going to be used, in terms of the length of head-shunts, run-round loops and sidings. Points are also important - you cannot have small-radius points and long 4-6-2 locomotives, but you can have small-radius points with short-wheelbase locos.

If you are modelling a specific prototype, certain allowances will have to be made to suit the site of the layout - what is sometimes called

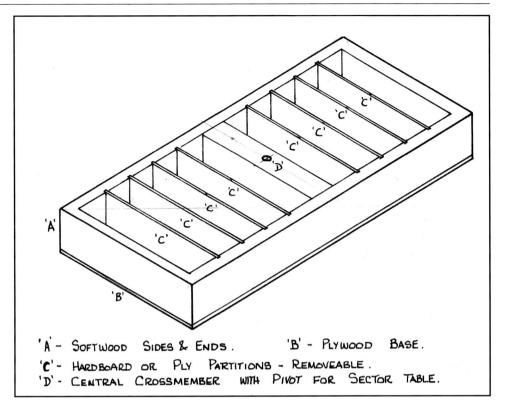

'A' – SOFTWOOD SIDES & ENDS.　　'B' – PLYWOOD BASE.
'C' – HARDBOARD OR PLY PARTITIONS – REMOVEABLE.
'D' – CENTRAL CROSSMEMBER WITH PIVOT FOR SECTOR TABLE.

'selective compression', ie reducing the length of the platform or leaving out a siding to avoid unacceptable widening or lengthening of the baseboard.

On the other hand you may, like me, wish to design a 'freelance' layout. This means that it is not a strict copy of a prototype location, but it is to be hoped that, when it is complete and operating, it looks convincing. Iain Rice's definition of a freelance layout is 'a model which, while accurate in each of it several respects, does not represent any one prototype location . . . this means that I usually select compatible elements from a number of prototype locations, and bring them together in a fictional arrangement, under a fictional title.'

Having decided whether the layout is to be based on a prototype or be freelance, you can get down to work. Obviously if it is the former, you can relatively easily finalise the visible part of the layout. I will deal with the fiddle yard later.

If the layout is freelance you can spend many happy hours making design sketches and plans. To do this you first need to check the length of the stock you are going to use; as I said earlier, this is crucial to the design. Clearly, you cannot run locomotives that are 16 inches long if you only have a 12-inch headshunt at the end of the run-round loop. Likewise, the tracks in the fiddle yard must be of approximately the same length as any run-round loop; it is not much good having a fiddle yard that allows you to put together a train 5 feet long if, when that train gets to the terminus, the run-round loop

only measures 4 feet. However, such a train would be acceptable if the layout was of the fiddle-yard-to-fiddle-yard variety, the fiddle yards were about the same length, and the train was running through from one to the other without stopping in a loop.

When you have got a plan that you think is what you want, I strongly recommend that you try it out at full size. I use lining paper, which you can buy cheaply at any of the large DIY retailers; it is approximately 21 inches wide and comes in rolls. Trying out your plan at full size has a number of advantages. You can

- see if it actually fits
- draw in any cross-bracing for the baseboard framework to avoid points
- double-check the positions of electrical feeds and dead sections
- place mock-up buildings (made from cardboard or cereal packets) on the plan to get an idea of the three-dimensional view of the layout, moving them about until you are satisfied
- place stock on the layout to check the lengths of run-round loops, fouling points, etc
- work out your sequence timetable in advance of laying any track, knowing that it will work
- make any alterations that prove to be necessary before any track is laid
- work out any necessary cross-baseboard connections, which is easier at full size, and discover where best to locate any electrical connectors

Drawing out your plan full size is particularly useful if you are intending to have more than one level, as you can draw out the top level plan separately and super-impose it on the lower level; this will also give an idea of the overall height of the baseboards including scenery.

If you model in O gauge, as I do, I suggest that it would pay to invest in pointwork paper templates (as supplied by Marcway and Peco) to use on your full-size plan. For example, a Marcway three-way point in 1996 is £35, and it would be a disaster to spend that sort of money only to find that the plan did not fit the area available and you had to redesign it. The Marcway templates cost £5 when I bought mine, and they can be reused time and again. Peco also supplies templates for other gauges.

I have found it worthwhile to invest in a couple of yards of track at the full-size-plan stage so that, for both straights and curves, you can use it as a template where necessary.

Another alternative at the planning stage, which I have used once, is to make a cardboard mock-up of the layout (say to a scale of 1 inch to 1 foot). This was a help, but in my opinion not as good as a full-size plan.

Fiddle yards

The fiddle yard represents the rest of the railway system, and is usually, though not always, hidden from view to enable trains to be made up, locos to be moved from one end to the other, and spare stock to be stored.

There are various types of fiddle yard:

- Fan of sidings using points. This is expensive both in terms of the cost of the points and in space, but some modellers nevertheless prefer this method. I have to say that for layouts in limited spaces it is not my favourite for space reasons alone, but I have used it once.
- Sector plate or sector table, which is a very common method - see the accompanying drawings, which I think are self-explanatory.
- A traverser - again, see the accompanying drawing. This method has the advantage that the locomotives need not be handled, as a spare road can be used to run round in the fiddle yard.
- Cassettes. This is the most recent method used for the hidden sidings. The cassettes can either be lifted out and stored on a table at the side of the layout, or can be stored in the hidden sidings area itself. In the latter case the surface can be Melamine-faced chipboard, and if the cassettes are of the same material, they slide easily over the main surface. The cassettes can be of different lengths, short for individual locos and longer for whole trains. They can also be joined together to feed into the main entry track. Cassettes can either have flexible track laid on them or, as used by many people, aluminium angle set carefully to the track gauge so that the angle itself effectively forms the track.

It used to be assumed that the fiddle yard would automatically be located at the end of the layout, whether the layout was straight or curved through 90 or 180 degrees. However, it is possible to place the fiddle yard behind the scenic part of the layout; this is quite commonly done on continuous layouts. (On larger layouts - beyond the scope of this book - the operators are located in the middle.) In the smaller scales (OO9 and N) the fiddle yard can easily be accommodated within the width of the baseboard. I did this on my OO9 layout 'The Milverton Light Railway',

A sector plate in use on the Fairbourne Railway. *Author*

Types of fiddle yards - sidings with points, sector plate and sector table - and (*bottom*) a traverser.

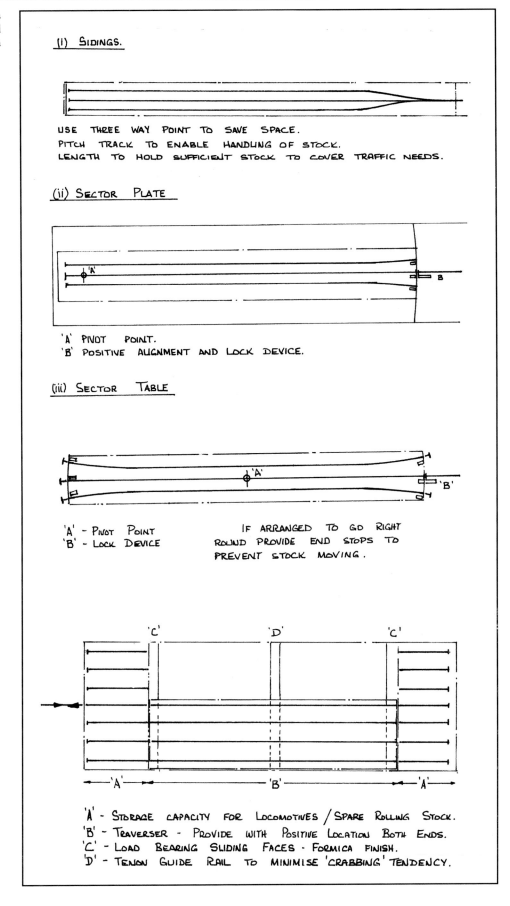

(i) SIDINGS.

USE THREE WAY POINT TO SAVE SPACE.
PITCH TRACK TO ENABLE HANDLING OF STOCK.
LENGTH TO HOLD SUFFICIENT STOCK TO COVER TRAFFIC NEEDS.

(ii) SECTOR PLATE

'A' PIVOT POINT.
'B' POSITIVE ALIGNMENT AND LOCK DEVICE.

(iii) SECTOR TABLE

'A' - PIVOT POINT
'B' - LOCK DEVICE

IF ARRANGED TO GO RIGHT ROUND PROVIDE END STOPS TO PREVENT STOCK MOVING.

'A' - STORAGE CAPACITY FOR LOCOMOTIVES / SPARE ROLLING STOCK.
'B' - TRAVERSER - PROVIDE WITH POSITIVE LOCATION BOTH ENDS.
'C' - LOAD BEARING SLIDING FACES - FORMICA FINISH.
'D' - TENON GUIDE RAIL TO MINIMISE 'CRABBING' TENDENCY.

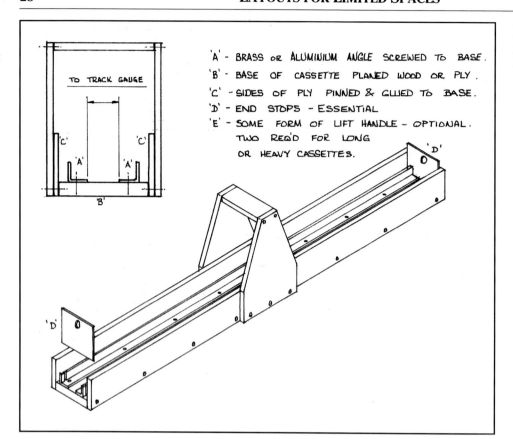

TO TRACK GAUGE

'A' - BRASS OR ALUMINIUM ANGLE SCREWED TO BASE.
'B' - BASE OF CASSETTE PLANED WOOD OR PLY.
'C' - SIDES OF PLY PINNED & GLUED TO BASE.
'D' - END STOPS - ESSENTIAL
'E' - SOME FORM OF LIFT HANDLE - OPTIONAL.
      TWO REQ'D FOR LONG
      OR HEAVY CASSETTES.

One design of stock cassette. Note that this one uses aluminium angle instead of conventional track.

An aerial view of one of Mike Hewitt's cassettes in position on the layout, showing the use of conventional track and the twin carrying handles. (See also the diagrams on page 102.) *Martin Hewitt*

which was on two levels. Gordon Gravett also did this in 0-16.5 on his Llandydref layout by using a 9-inch radius on a 24-inch-wide baseboard. However, it is also possible to put the hidden sidings behind the scenic part and join them to the scenic part by means of a sector plate. Dave Lowery did this (was he the first?) with his Bevet layout. As with all good ideas it is stunningly simple and works well. I followed his example with my 0-16.5 layout 'The Shed', and Bob Haskins did it with his layout Bayards Dock.

Finally on the subject of fiddle yards, it is possible to extend the size while the layout in use, yet keep them to the minimum size for transport. For example, if the chosen module length for all the baseboards of a layout is 36 inches but it is necessary to have 42-inch fiddle yards, it is possible to arrange a 6-inch extension as shown in the diagram on page 31. Thus enables the carrying crate to carry boards of the same length, but in use the fiddle yards are slightly longer.

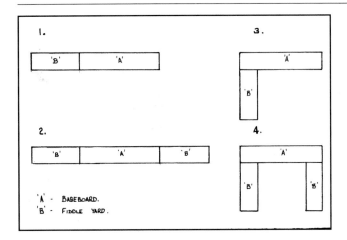

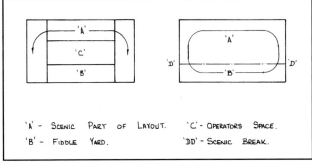

'A' - SCENIC PART OF LAYOUT.   'C' - OPERATORS SPACE.
'B' - FIDDLE YARD.   'DD' - SCENIC BREAK.

Above Accommodating the fiddle yard on a continuous layout.

Left Fiddle yard positions on end-to-end layouts.

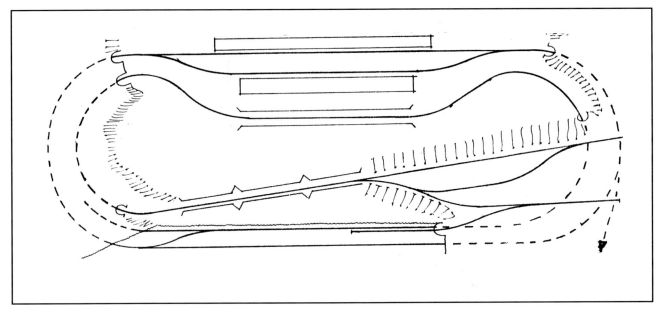

Above and right The Milverton Light Railway. The plan shows the accommodation of hidden sidings at both levels within the width of the layout, while the photograph shows Riversleigh Halt, at the front of the layout. *Photo Joe Prestidge*

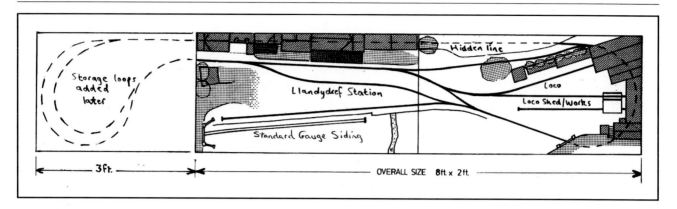

Above and left Plan of Gordon Gravett's Llandydref layout, showing the hidden line curving behind the back of the layout. The photograph shows *Margaret* and train arriving at the station while *Falcon* shunts empty slate wagons in the exchange siding. The station buildings mask the hidden line. *Gordon Gravett*

Left A view of the locos on my 7 mm narrow gauge layout 'The Shed'. Note the loco coming on to the turntable and the men working in the entrance to the yard. *Barry Poultney*

Right and below right Dave Lowery's Bevet, showing the use of a sector plate to connect hidden sidings with the layout. The photograph shows a general view of the station with the scenic background that conceals the sidings. *Dave Lowery*

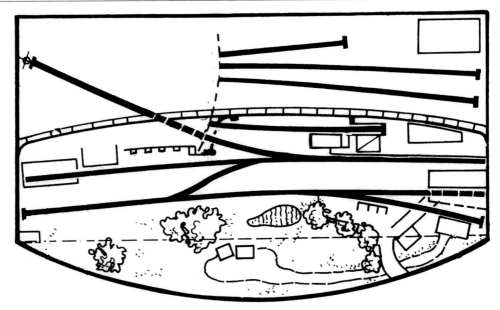

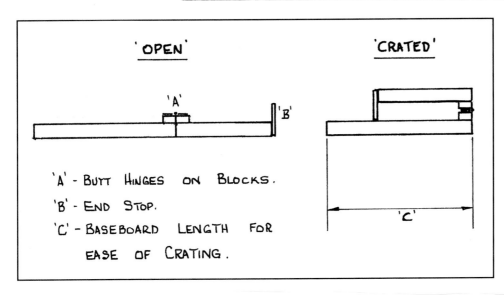

'OPEN' 'CRATED'

'A' - BUTT HINGES ON BLOCKS.

'B' - END STOP.

'C' - BASEBOARD LENGTH FOR EASE OF CRATING.

Extending the fiddle yard.

Layout supports

At exhibitions the layout can be supported in a number of ways. One is the simple trestle. I have three trestles built over 16 years ago, which have seen sterling service. They are very simple to design and carry, and the legs are held apart by a metal gate strut. This is very important, because I remember operating someone else's layout at an exhibition when the trestle legs where held apart by rope. Unfortunately a member of the public accidentally knocked one of the legs and the trestle folded up! Thankfully the spare operator was standing at that end of the layout and caught it.

Another design of trestle was used to support Keith Foster's Melison Bridge layout back in the late '70s; this had three legs.

Justin's layout in the loft is supported by a Dexion angle-iron frame. This is very rigid, but erecting the framework would be too time-consuming at shows.

Another method of supporting a layout is to provide it with bolt-on legs and struts. We used this method once, but changed to trestles because they took less time when setting up at shows.

Depending on the length and width of the baseboard it is possible to support a layout on a folding ironing-board. In the 1960s I built an 009 layout on an ironing-board (see Chapter 7). The same principle could be used to support wider baseboards simple by fitting 'outriggers'. The ironing-board has the great advantage of being easily carried, and takes up very little space because it folds flat.

Finally there are folding legs. These can be incorporated in the baseboard framework itself, or they can be part of a sep-

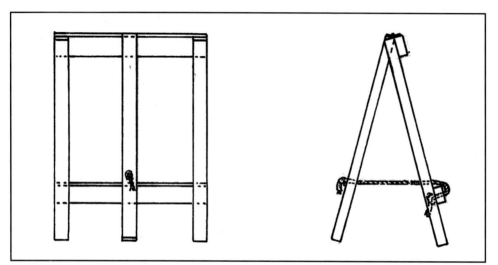

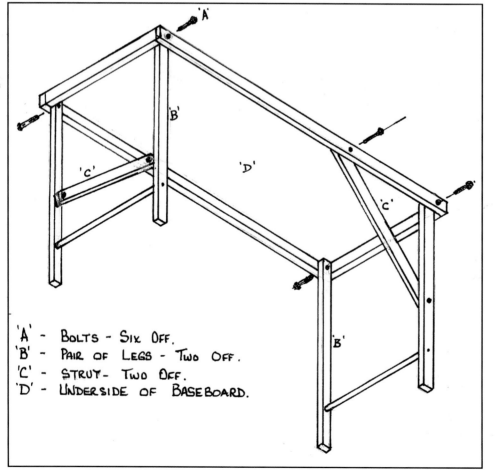

'A' – BOLTS – SIX OFF.
'B' – PAIR OF LEGS – TWO OFF.
'C' – STRUT – TWO OFF.
'D' – UNDERSIDE OF BASEBOARD.

Above left The three-legged trestle.

Left A layout support framework with bolt-on legs and struts.

Right Using an ironing-board as a layout support.

Below right Hinged legs with folding struts.

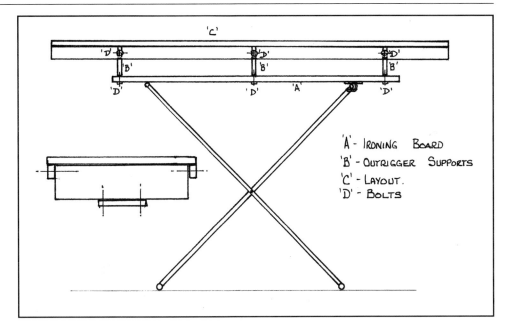

'A' - IRONING BOARD
'B' - OUTRIGGER SUPPORTS
'C' - LAYOUT.
'D' - BOLTS

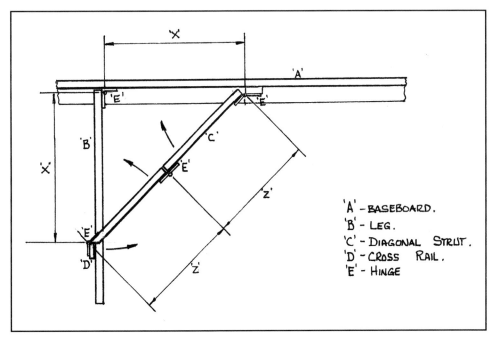

'A' - BASEBOARD.
'B' - LEG.
'C' - DIAGONAL STRUT.
'D' - CROSS RAIL.
'E' - HINGE

arate framework as on my MPD layout. This framework was designed and made for me by one of my parishioners, and is very ingenious (see the photographs on page 34).

Metal trestles can be bought ready made. I was lucky enough to be in our local DIY superstore recently when they were selling some off cheaply, so I immediately bought four to replace our ageing wooden trestles. They are very sturdily made and stack together very easily. Once again, they are multi-purpose - they can be used for two of my O gauge layouts and both of Justin's OO layouts.

One factor is crucial, and that is the height at which the layout will be shown at exhibitions. There are those who feel that the layout should be shown at a height of about 5 feet so that people can get an 'eye-level' view. That's all very well if you're an adult of about 5 ft 10 in, but I have to say that I very much disagree with layouts being at that height. It bars children completely from seeing them, and many adults as well, especially any in wheelchairs. I am 5 ft 8 in tall, have tried to look at such layouts at exhibitions and have given up. The operators also seem tacitly to admit that most people can't see, because they control the layout from a raised walkway - more to carry! Moreover, exhibiting layouts at such a height effectively prohibits the use of folding legs within the baseboard framework unless the baseboard is slightly longer than the height of the folding legs.

Electrics and point control

I will not dwell on this subject but a number of issues need to be mentioned in connection with layouts in limited spaces.

First, if the layout is on one baseboard, all the controls can be incorporated into that board and all that has to be connected is the 16V AC and the 12V DC. Do *not* have mains electricity (240V) within the main baseboard framework. I always put my transformer on the floor under the layout and simply take two wires up to the layout.

If you prefer to be able to operate the layout from

An ingenious folding support frame with centre support to prevent collapse. The photographs show the frame fully folded, on its side with the three support elements being unfolded, and fully erected ready to take the layout with the centre support screwed into the underside of the centre cross-brace. Since these photographs were taken the framework has been stained both for looks and protection.
Martin Hewitt

both front and back, it is quite possible to have all the switches in a detachable box, which can be hung in the baseboard framework. If you do this remember to fit a DPDT (double-pole, double-throw) switch in the main 12V DC supply so that the direction of travel is reversed when you swap from front to back, as you will have turned the box through 180 degrees.

If there is more than one baseboard, connections have to be made between them. The easiest way of doing this is through multi-pin plugs and sockets; there is a bewildering variety of these. You can either put the plug on one board and the socket in the other, or you can put a socket on each board and join them with a detachable lead with a plug on each end, which avoids the risk of damaging the leads in transit by pulling them off accidentally, but it obviously doubles the number of plugs and sockets needed. DIN plugs and sockets can be used in the same way. One way of minimising the number of cross-baseboard connections is to situate control panels on each baseboard. This can be done in such a way that, when the layout is erected, the panels are adjacent to one another.

Controllers themselves can be built into the panel, as I have done on a number of occasions. The disadvantage, of course, is that should the controller fail you

Above right Using a detachable control panel at both sides of the layout.

Right The control panel on my small 7 mm MPD layout. It is totally self-contained and only requires two plugs in the two 'AC in' sockets on the right-hand side. In case the built-in controller fails, provision is made for a hand-held one to be plugged into the DIN socket at the front of the panel. The DPDT switch above the main controller controls which is 'live'. *Martin Hewitt*

have a problem! I overcome this by fitting a DPDT switch in the supply, allowing me to use a walk-around controller that fits into a DIN socket on the panel, as shown in the accompanying photograph.

When it comes to points, although I have used motors on occasions, I usually tend to keep it simple and use hand-operated methods, including those shown in the accompanying diagram. All are effective in their own way.

To ensure that you do not rely on point-blade contact for electrical continuity, you can fit micro-switches or solder wires to relevant rails on the point and take them to the separate switches. I have used this method quite successfully, but if the two elements

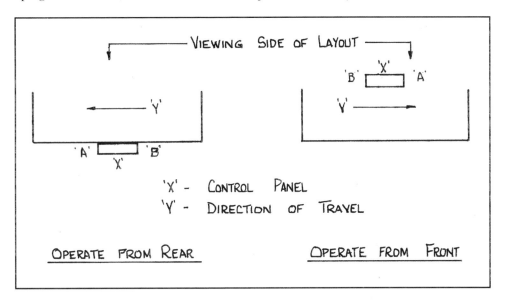

are separate you have to remember to pull or push the lever *and* operate the switch. Another method is to connect the pull-push rod to the black plastic switch of a slide switch. In this way, when you move the switch you move the point and change the polarity at the same time.

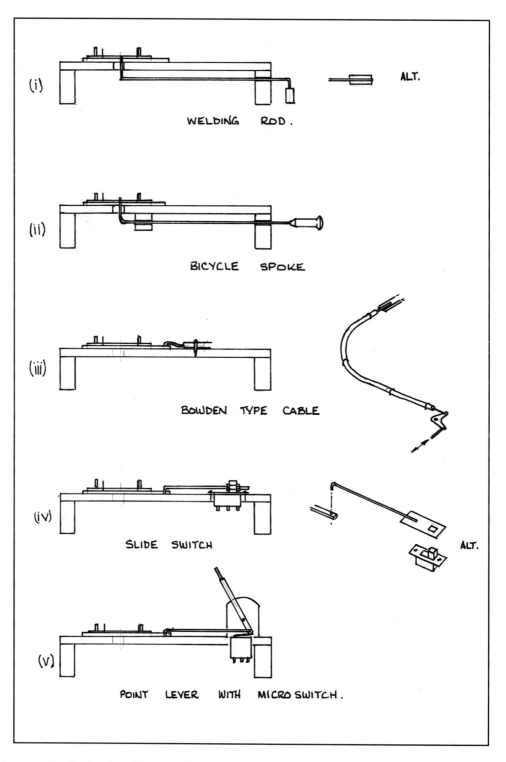

(i) WELDING ROD. ALT.

(ii) BICYCLE SPOKE

(iii) BOWDEN TYPE CABLE

(iv) SLIDE SWITCH ALT.

(v) POINT LEVER WITH MICRO SWITCH.

Methods of point operation by hand: welding wire bent at 90 degrees at each end; bicycle spokes; car choke or heater cable (Bowden cable); and slide switch or lever connected to the tie-bar by wire or wire in a tube. Note the lever attached to a micro-switch to ensure electrical connection more effectively that by point-blade contact alone.

4.
SCENERY

I believe that small layouts must be strong on scenery and detail so that the attention of the viewing public is held when the movement of rolling-stock stops to allow for work in the fiddle yard. Also, because the layouts are small and can be completed reasonably quickly, there is far more time available to build scenery and add detail.

The scenery depends to a very large extent on the type of layout being modelled. If it is a Welsh quarry layout, the dominant feature may well be slate heaps, and in the yard the tracks will be covered with slate debris. If it is a simple branch line, there may be a single line meandering through fields until it arrives at the terminus, which may have a very spacious feel to it because it has relatively little track and small buildings. Or the main feature on the layout might be an engine shed, approached alongside a grubby retaining wall. Indeed, there are many different types of retaining wall. For example, on the Talyllyn Railway there is a length of rail-built 'wall' to hold back a cutting side, which would be easy to model.

Whatever your layout, take a good look at the real thing and build accordingly. Let us take a

simple item - ballast. If you are modelling a well-used line, the ballast can look new and have proper shoulders and drainage channels. However, if the line has seen better days, the ballast will have grass and weeds growing up through it, the shoulders will not be so pronounced and there will be a general air of dilapidation. Alternatively, if you are modelling an engine shed, as I have done on a number of occasions, there will be hardly any ballast visible because the track and sleepers are buried in ash and cinders.

It is also true that the scenery can dictate the detail. For example, on two of my MPD layouts I built a very dilapidated fence along the front of the model. The resultant prominence of the fence meant that detail could include people working on it and repairing it, so amongst the detail there are new panels, tools, etc.

A rail-built 'retaining wall' on the Talyllyn Railway in Wharf Cutting just before the line goes under School Bridge into Pendre. Some pieces of Plasticard suitably cut and painted to represent the slate behind the rail would complete the picture. *Author*

Newport (IOW) shed on 24 March 1950. There is a wealth of detail for the modeller in this picture: the lifting gantry, the small wheels, the bits of sleepers, the lamp attached to the telegraph pole. Note also that the sleepers are almost entirely buried in 'gunge', which I model using Polyfilla; the puddles can also be effectively modelled. *Neil Davenport*

A layout where a dilapidated fence has been used to good effect. The old planks have been removed and a carpenter is in the process of replacing them. Some new planks are leaning against the buffer stop. *Martin Hewitt*

A more modern style of fence, complete with modern graffiti! One of the problems of graffiti is that it can 'date' a layout - I once had a layout with graffiti referring to Neil Kinnock and Margaret Thatcher, which was topical when written but would not be now. *Martin Hewitt*

On my small O gauge MPD I decided to portray a different type of fence, this time the SR concrete panels produced by Ratio. I tried to create the impression that this had been newly erected and, at the end nearest the traverser, it is clear that the job is not quite finished. However, not to be outdone the local graffiti artists (actually my younger son Paul) have already been along and made their mark! Such scenes 'ring bells' with people's own experiences, confirmed by comments made by members of the public at exhibitions.

Another item of detail that brings a layout to life is posters. There are a number of companies that produce excellent posters in a variety of scales and, suitably placed, they look very effective. But posters and signs do not always have to be on a wall. One of the most effective scenes I have made came from an American model railway magazine lent to me by a parishioner. The modeller had taken the model metal signs, mounted them on plasticard then stacked them on end against the wall outside a factory. I did the same, albeit with many fewer signs, but they still looked very effective.

People often say that you can see the same backscenes on a number of layouts on the exhibition circuit. This is true, but with a pair of scissors and a bit of imagination you can cut up proprietary backscenes and reposition the various elements to make them look different. I did this on two of my current layouts, The Shed and The MPD. On the former I was able to make a longish factory without simply repeating the backscene again, while on the latter I was able to make the buildings look different by cutting out pieces to block off windows, etc. I saw one layout on the exhibition circuit where the whole of the backscene was made up from pictures (from calendars, for example) suitably cut and stuck together, and very effective it was too.

There are often small areas of a layout on which a particular scenic feature can be built - allotments, for example. You do not need a large

area to model a small allotment, and they are seen in both city and countryside. On Justin's Brookhurst layout, started when he was eight years old, there were some allotments that, even at that age, he really enjoyed making. If you want to see allotments exquisitely modelled, go to the Pendon Museum at Long Wittenham near Didcot.

Another easy feature to model is a scrapyard. Again, they are commonly seen, and can be rail-served. When Justin was 12 he built an extension to his layout to make it L-shaped. The major scenic feature on the corner board was a scrapyard, and it won him third prize in the Junior Railway Modellers Competition in 1983.

When arranging the scenery it is a good idea to make little cameos to attract people's attention. At exhibitions we have found that when we display a list of various detail items under the heading 'Can you spot. . .?', members of the public will spend ages looking for them. For example, some of the items on Justin's Brookhurst Stabling Point layout that viewers are asked to spot are

- a man working under a car in the car park
- a bicycle leaning against the wall of a hut
- two dustbins with lids off and rubbish inside
- men digging a hole
- a man opening the rear door of a van
- a man working to repair a colour light signal

This gives a flavour of what I mean by scenic detail. It can take many forms, and a number of specialised

The allotments on Justin's Brookhurst layout, which he built with help from me when he was eight years old. They were a feature often commented on by the public at exhibitions. *Birmingham Post*

manufacturers produce detailed bits and pieces including buildings, fences, posters, platform 'furniture' (seats, trolleys, weighing machines, tools) and, of course, people. I think miniature figures are vital if the scenic side of the layout is to come alive.

One of the most successful layouts I have built was an OO9 MPD measuring 36 by 20 inches; it had over 100 figures on it, but they did not look out of place.

There are a wide variety of figures available today in all the main scales, and some of them are in specific 'poses' (eg man carrying a ladder), so you can build up little cameos. These could include a man changing a wheel on a car or a road-mending gang, complete with the worker who is leaning on his broom watching the others work and the foreman giving instructions! All these little scenes bring the small layout to life and create talking points for those who are watching.

The type of layout chosen can also help bring it to life with movement. I don't mean just the movement of the stock, but things like operating level crossing gates, a gate to a private siding that opens and closes, a traverser or a turntable. I have used all of these at one time or another and they are guaranteed to hold the viewer's attention. Traversers and turntables have another big advantage if you are operating a layout at an exhibition. You can set them to move slowly, and while they are moving to the required position, you can have a quick drink or a bite to eat!

On the basis that a picture is worth a thousand words, I have included a selection of photographs showing scenic details on models that I and other modellers have built, and some prototype detail, taken mainly on the Talyllyn Railway. From these photographs you will see why I think that the smaller the layout the more detail it needs in order to impress viewers and hold their attention. Often it's the women who stop and admire the detail.

Left Justin extended his Brookhurst layout by making it L-shaped, and the resulting corner board featured a scrapyard, the detail for which came from various sources. The material in the yard was arranged to look like a typical scrapyard, which is not quite so easy as it might seem. *Joe Prestidge, courtesy* Railway Modeller

Below left This photograph of Gordon Gravett's 7 mm Ditchling Green layout sums up what I have been saying about scenic detail. The small signal cabin is modelled on the prototype at Hayling Island, while the road vehicles are rebuilt die-cast models from Corgi and Dinky. But look at all the other detail - the signal, the fence, the cabbages by the signal box, the point rodding, the footboard, the fire buckets, the end wall of the station building, and the narrow gauge track behind the fence. The etched fence has been improved by thickening the posts and rails with lengths of stretched fuse wire soldered on. This picture was shown to a friend who though it was the real thing, which says it all. *Gordon Gravett*

Another view of Ditchling Green, showing the gated crossing where the industrial tramway crosses the standard gauge tracks. The fencing, the cast iron signs and the gate are particularly effective. *Gordon Gravett*

A view of my small MPD layout, showing again how attention to detail can add to the general picture. There are many scenic details, and it is these that the viewing public see because the area they are looking at is so much smaller than on a large layout; their viewing is very much more concentrated into a small area. The layout uses a traverser, which provides almost continuous movement. *Martin Hewitt*

The 009 MPD I built in 1973, bustling with life. Airfix infantrymen have been used as workmen on the roof. The hut immediately behind the turntable hides a point motor. *Brian Higgins*

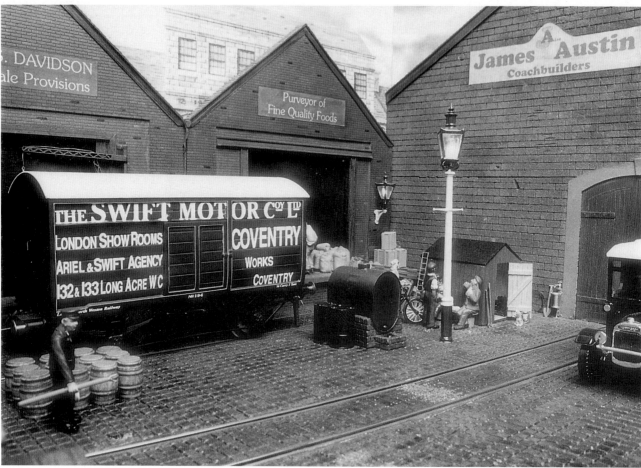

Above left Geraint Hughes's Middlepeak Wharf, a superb example of detail on a layout. Look at the bridge in the foreground, the notice warning people not to cross the line, the notice on the wall of the small shed, the long grass, the water and the walkway right across the tracks. *Railway Modeller*

Left Mike Hewitt's Gas Street Yard; note the superb van at the unloading platform. *Martin Hewitt*

Top A close-up of the area around the small shed. Note the dog, the bike, and the tools leaning against the shed - all so true to life. *Martin Hewitt*

Above The station building and goods shed on my Brynglas layout. Note the men changing the wheel on the coal lorry watched by a man on his bike. *Barry Poultney*

The following prototype detail photographs show a variety of ideas that could be modelled. The majority were taken on the Talyllyn Railway, where I am a volunteer, but they could apply to any railway.

Left The first shows the ground frame at Tywyn Wharf. Note the wooden platform made from sleepers, and the drainage holes in the retaining wall of the road overbridge - the latter can be modelled using drinking straws.

Above left Fire-irons hanging near the ash pit at Pendre shed. Note the wood and brick construction of the shed.

Above Why should all lamps go down to the ground? This example is next to the level crossing at Tywyn Pendre; in modelling terms the wiring could easily be taken up inside the supporting slate wall.

Left Metal storage racks fixed to the wall of the south shed at Pendre, with a short lean-to roof above.

A tank mounted on sleepers on Tywyn, Wharf Edge, together with an upturned wheelbarrow and various wheelsets. Note the long grass and the weeds growing round the various items.

The track in 'Tadpole Cutting' just above Brynglas. Note the 'Whistle' board and the comparison between the newly strimmed grass on the right and the uncut grass on the left.

All photos by the author

Finally, this photograph shows the refuelling point at Machynlleth station on the Shrewsbury-Aberystwyth line. Here there is a wealth of detail for the modern image mod-eller: the wagons, the storage tank with the brick wall around it, and the various pipes and cans. Note also the rock face behind the siding.

5.
ROLLING-STOCK AND OPERATION

Rolling-stock

As I said in the chapter on designing small layouts, it is crucial to the operational success of the layout that it is designed with the stock in mind. If you do not know what locos you are going to use at this stage, manufacturers and retailers are usually very helpful and will either supply the information you need or let you measure locos in the shop.

In my case, when I built my first 7 mm standard gauge layout I had already bought a couple of Lima 0-4-0 diesel shunters to see what they were like. You can work wonders with these simply by repainting them; fortunately for me, Mike Hewitt is a member of COVGOG, and he repainted two for me. The difference is fantastic, but even without these skills a

straightforward repaint in plain green is well worth while. You can also repaint and/or modify Atlas diesel shunters; these are particularly good runners because of the large weight inside them.

Both Lima and Atlas chassis can be used under kit or scratchbuilt locos. For instance, I have three tram locos made from Highfield kits and all are powered by Lima diesel chassis, as are two Highfield Sentinel loco kits. An Atlas diesel chassis is used to power a scratchbuilt loco based on a Wisbech & Upwell Tramway prototype; both of these I bought second-hand.

'Entertainment' locos can also be made for use at exhibitions. Ertl produces a push-along model of *Percy* (the Green Engine in Revd W. Awdry's books). I have motorised one of these by using a Lima 0-4-0 chassis and it certainly is a hit with the children at shows, as is *Toby* with his face on each end made with Milliput.

I have found that most locomotives liable to be used on a small O gauge layout are about 8 inches long, and this is a good guide. By the same token, if the layout you wish to build is going to use a lot of wagons, you will need to know the length of them so that siding lengths and head-shunts can be of the required length. Again, a good guide to length is

An Atlas diesel and another Highfield tram loco on my Shed layout. The Hinckley Times

6 inches. As with locos, manufacturers and retailers can be helpful with pre-purchase measurements, although it is often the case that layout builders already have stock that they can measure.

It is not impossible to run larger locomotives on a small layout if the layout is of the correct type. For example, I am currently building another O gauge layout, and although it is only 9 ft 6 in long it will take Lima Class 33s, which are about 13.5 inches long over the buffers.

A glance through any of the railway modelling magazines will show you plenty of examples of short-wheelbase locomotives and rolling-stock, as will visits to trade stands at exhibitions. You can also make your own short-wheelbase stock using a proprietary chassis. I have taken the chassis from an O gauge Lima GWR

Above right A close-up of *Toby* showing his Milliput face. *Tony Wright*

No 5 *Midlander* stands on a siding with the Talyllyn Railway's weed-killing train; the tanks on the 'Boflat' contain the weed-killing solution. Note the greenery growing over the boundary fence from the bungalows behind, a feature not very often modelled. *Author*

An 0-16.5 loco made by converting a Triang Hornby Caledonian 0-4-0 loco. *Joe Prestidge*

Another conversion, this time from a Lima HO diesel and spare parts from other conversions of the same loco. *Joe Prestidge*

brake-van and made it into a works wagon loaded with a tool box and various bits and pieces. I think it looks quite attractive and is certainly something different.

Narrow gauge modelling provides the opportunity to have short locomotives and stock and to build freelance items if you wish (a prototype narrow gauge example, the Talyllyn Railway's weed-killing train, is shown in the photograph on page 47). I did this when I modelled in 0-16.5, again as shown in the photographs.

Clearly, if you model in N gauge, or even in Z gauge, there is ample opportunity to run larger locomotives and rolling-stock on a layout that will still go into a limited space, but the choice of gauge will have been made long before you reach the design stage. Some people use the smaller gauges so that their layout is correspondingly smaller, so it is not always the case that modellers pick the smaller gauges to squeeze in as much as they can into the space available.

The wheelbase of the locomotives is of paramount importance if there are to be sharp curves on the layout. For instance, on his 0-16.5 layout 'Llandyref', Gordon Gravett found that the locomotives he was going to use would go round a very tight radius, so there was absolutely no problem in having a curve of 9 inches in the hidden sidings.

Operating methods

It is vital the small layouts are interesting to operate, otherwise the operator will get bored and lose interest. Exceptions are perhaps the very simple small lay-outs, but these are usually either operated automatically or come into what I will call the 'gimmick' category. Included in the latter are what are sometimes called 'tail-chasing' layouts, which have been fitted into an old TV cabinet, for example. Such layouts, especially if well-built and attractive, are often a talking-point at an exhibition, but do not offer interesting operational possibilities!

It is, of course, entirely possible to just 'play trains' with the layout with no plan of operation at all, but I have to admit it is not for me.

Essentially there are six basic methods of operating a small layout:

- shunting around the layout using wagons differentiated by coloured pins and positioning them to match coloured pins located at various places
- a tape-recorded commentary (as on Les Eden's Bossington layout in the late 1960s and early 1970s)
- a sequence programmed into a computer and displayed on a screen for public and operators to see
- a sequence written out on cards and worked to a speeded-up clock
- a sequence written out on cards that may or may not also be displayed to the public
- a sequence, also written out on cards, but having imaginary connections with other stations and drawn out on a graph (as happens on the Talyllyn Railway) to make sure it all works. The cards may be visible the public. This is really a development of the previous method.

All except the first method can involve more than one operator, depending on where the fiddle yard is. Let us look at them each in turn.

Shunting using coloured pins

This entails fitting coloured pins to each item of rolling-stock - usually on the operator's side of the layout - and putting various coloured pins in position on the layout itself. A train is then made up in the fiddle yard and sent out on to the main layout, where the operator shunts the wagons so that the coloured pins match up. Conversely, to get the train back into the fiddle yard the wagons are coupled back together and depart. I have to admit never having used this method personally, but I have seen it used at exhibitions.

Tape-recorded commentary

The success of this method relies crucially on the making of the commentary tape. The secret is to build in 'recovery time' and time for shunting and running round, etc, by describing buildings, rolling-stock, or an imaginary history of the line.

The first time I experienced this method was on Les Eden's Bossington Branch in the late 1960s. Bossington was a simple fiddle-yard-to-GWR-terminus layout; to operate it at shows was great fun and the commentary always attracted a crowd, even if, at a long show, it probably drove other exhibitors nearby round the bend!

While John Pomroy's Winton layout is probably outside the scope of this book, he developed the tape-recorded commentary further for an end-to-end layout of some size, and the build-up to the arrival of the 'Silver Jubilee' express at the end of the sequence never failed to excite operators and the viewing public alike.

If you are prepared to spend the time making the tape, timing movements and practising operating to the tape, it can be very satisfying for both operator and spectator.

Sequence programmed into a computer

The complexities of this method are really beyond the scope of this book, and it will only appeal to the serious, computer-literate modeller, who is referred to specialist books and magazine articles on the subject! All I can say is that I have seen it at work at shows, and for those who are able to do it, it is very effective.

Sequences written out on cards

Of the various 'card sequence' methods, my favourite is the sequence timetable. I have never used the speeded-up clock method myself - I know that it does work, but you need the sequence first. Neither have I worked out imaginary connections to other stations by using a graph, but I have done it in real life on occasions when working out paths for special trains on the Talyllyn Railway, on which I volunteer. The real thing can be very satisfying, and no doubt those who use this method for their model railways find it equally so. Certainly I remember articles in the *Railway Modeller* back in the 1950s or '60s by John Charman in which he described how he used the graph method to work out the timetable sequence for his Charford branch.

Using the Talyllyn graph reproduced here as an example, it can be seen that the stations are listed on the vertical axis and the times on the horizontal axis. The times shown are part of the actual train service for June 1995, and I am indebted to the TR for

A Talyllyn Railway train graph. Places and distances in miles are shown on the vertical axis, with time being shown on the horizontal axis. Solid lines across the graph under a station name indicate a passing loop facility; the remainder is single line. *Talyllyn Railway*

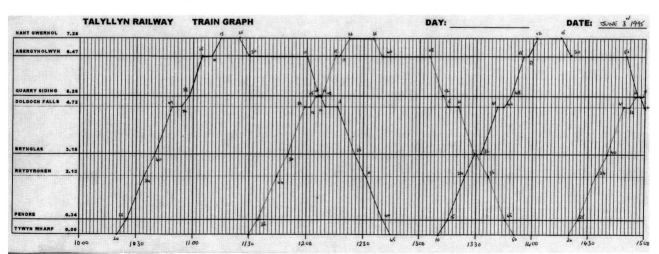

allowing me to use this information and the graph sheet. Being a single-line railway with passing loops, the TR's graph has to be planned in such a way that crossings can only happen at the loops - otherwise disaster ensues! Note, for example, that the 11.30 from Tywyn Wharf crosses with the 12.00 from Abergynolwyn at Quarry Siding between 12.05 and 12.08.

Having planned the graph and proved it works, the working timetable can be compiled from it, as happens in real life. Let me now explain in detail my own method of working out a sequence.

Compiling a sequence of operations

On pages 65-67 I describe my 0-16.5 Motive Power Depot layout. This was built mainly for exhibitions and, as can be seen from the accompanying track plan, it was simply an MPD fed from a pivoted fiddle yard.

It might be said that it is impossible to have a sequence of operations for a layout such as this because it has no station or goods yard or any of the usual facilities normally found on a more conventional layout. I hope to prove that this is not so, and that it is in fact possible to have the best of both worlds: a layout on which one can aimlessly 'play trains' by moving locos around at will, *or* a layout that is operated to a pre-planned sequence. I prefer the latter, of course, particularly for exhibitions.

There are various methods of compiling timetables, but the following example seems to suit me and the layouts I have built over the past few years.

To start with you need a marked-up track plan to identify every possible parking place for a loco (see the second diagram). This is simply to ensure that the operator can identify where their various places are; in the case of my MPD, this was very basic.

Next you get a big sheet of paper (I use A3 graph paper because it already has horizontal and vertical lines) and draw on it a chart as shown in the third diagram. From this you will see that there is a column for every loco parking place and room to describe each movement that you make.

Before you can plan any moves, you need to know where every item of stock is on the layout, and for this use the 'Start of sequence' top row in the diagram. Then describe each move in the 'Movement' column, eg 'A1 to E1', and make the move on the chart by writing in 'EMPTY' or a zero in the column for the location that the loco has left, and 'LOCO' or 'L' in the column to which it has moved. As a double-check you can also make the move on the chart shown in the fourth diagram by crossing out the 'L' on the parking place where the loco started from and replacing it with a dash (-). The movement is then traced out on the plan and an 'L' is marked at the new parking place.

This tracing out is important as I found the hard way! I was merrily crossing out the 'L' and moving it to its new location when I realised that I was trying to put locos into the fiddle yard, which was impossible. I had forgotten that I already had a loco parked in road K (the only access to the fiddle yard)! So I had to start all over again. This process continues until you feel you have a sequence that is long enough for your requirements.

In planning the moves you must remember that the disposition should be the same at the end of the sequence as it was at the beginning, so that the operations can sim-

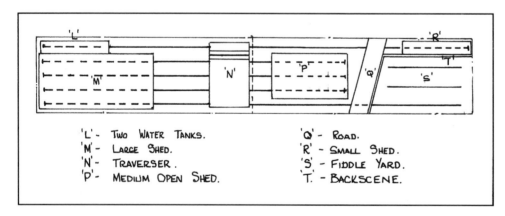

'L' - TWO WATER TANKS.
'M' - LARGE SHED.
'N' - TRAVERSER.
'P' - MEDIUM OPEN SHED.
'Q' - ROAD.
'R' - SMALL SHED.
'S' - FIDDLE YARD.
'T' - BACKSCENE.

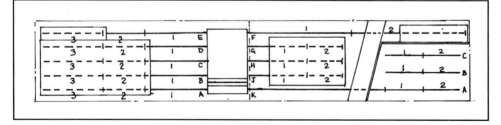

Above left The 0-16.5 MPD layout.

Left Diagram showing the 'parking places' on the layout, by numbered position per lettered track.

Right Movement chart before the details of the movements are entered.

Below right Chart of the parking positions allowing double-checking of loco movements. '0' indicates an empty place, 'L' indicates that it is occupied by a loco.

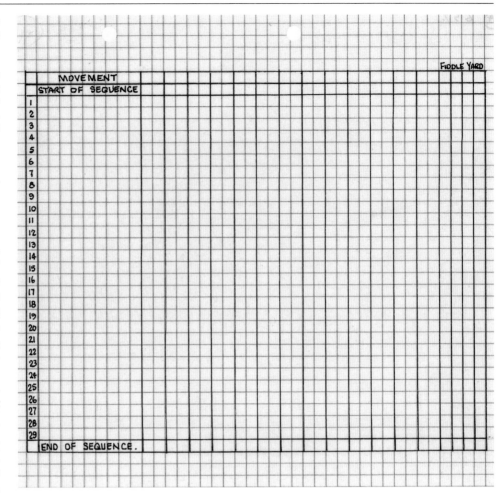

ply carry on without any need for 'hand shunting'. (If you have a conventional terminus-to-fiddle-yard layout and you do not have a sector plate at the end of the fiddle yard, or some other means of moving the loco back to the front of the train, this will have to be done by hand.)

You have now completed your planning of the moves, and the completed chart is shown here. To double-check I always retrace all of the moves on the layout plan again, which I think is worth while.

At this stage you can also run through the sequence on the layout itself, and if you are completely happy you can proceed to the next stage, which is to write out a card for each move.

Each card carries the number of the move, and mine are all mounted in an old ring-binder base, which is screwed to a piece of wood that is slightly larger than the cards.

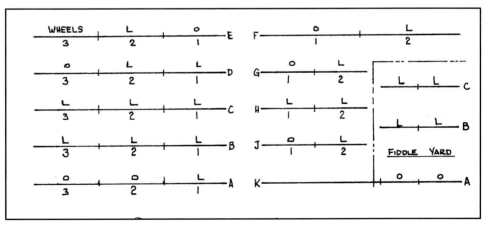

The cards are punched to fit into the binder rings, and the whole thing is fixed to the layout in such a way that when the operator's card is turned over, the next movement is written on the back for spectators to see, assuming that the writing or typing is large enough.

Each card should contain the minimum of information to allow the move to be made (see the accompanying examples), otherwise the operator will spend

too long trying to understand what he is supposed to be doing.

This method of compiling a sequence of operations enables the layout to be operated in an orderly fashion, it makes life easier for the operator in that the moves are all pre-planned, and, more importantly, if any questions are asked by members of the public at exhibitions, and they usually are, at worst you only have to finish one move before answering rather than having to wait until the end of a complete timetable.

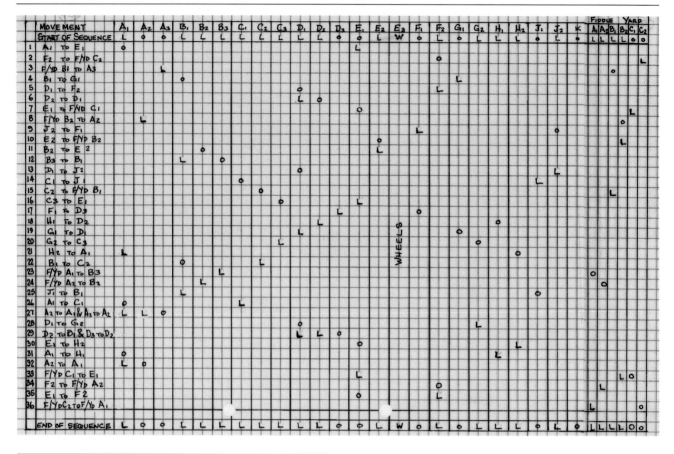

	MOVEMENT	A_1	A_2	A_3	B_1	B_2	B_3	C_1	C_2	C_3	D_1	D_2	D_3	E_1	E_2	E_3	F_1	F_2	G_1	G_2	H_1	H_2	J_1	J_2	K	FIDDLE YARD A_1	A_2	B_1	B_2	C_1	C_2
	START OF SEQUENCE	L	o	o	L	L	L	L	L	L	L	L	o	o	L	W	o	L	o	L	L	L	o	L	o	L	L	L	L	o	o
1	A_1 TO E_1	o												L																	
2	F_2 TO F/YD C_2																	o													L
3	F/YD B1 TO A3			L																								o			
4	B_1 TO G_1				o														L												
5	D_1 TO F_2										o							L													
6	D_2 TO D_1										L	o																			
7	E_1 TO F/YD C_1													o																L	
8	F/YD B_2 TO A_2		L																										o		
9	J_2 TO F_1																L							o							
10	E2 TO F/YD B2														o														L		
11	B2 TO E 2					o									L																
12	B_3 TO B_1				L		o																								
13	D_1 TO J2										o													L							
14	C1 TO J1							o															L								
15	C2 TO F/YD B_1								o																			L			
16	C3 TO E_1									o				L																	
17	F_1 TO D3												L				o														
18	H_1 TO D2											L									o										
19	G1 TO D_1										L								o												
20	G2 TO C3									L						WHEELS				o											
21	H2 TO A_1	L																				o									
22	B_1 TO C2				o				L																						
23	F/YD A_1 TO B3						L																			o					
24	F/YD A2 TO B2					L																					o				
25	J_1 TO B_1				L																		o								
26	A1 TO C_1	o						L																							
27	A2 TO A_1 & A_3 TO A_2	L	L	o																											
28	D_1 TO G2										o									L											
29	D2 TO D_1 & D3 TO D_2										L	L	o																		
30	E_1 TO H2													o								L									
31	A_1 TO H_1	o																			L										
32	A2 TO A_1	L	o																												
33	F/YD C_1 TO E_1													L															L	o	
34	F2 TO F/YD A2																	o									L				
35	E1 TO F2													o				L													
36	F/YD C2 TO F/YD A_1																									L					o
	END OF SEQUENCE	L	o	o	L	L	L	L	L	L	L	L	o	o	L	W	o	L	o	L	L	L	o	L	o	L	L	L	L	o	o

Above The completed movement chart.

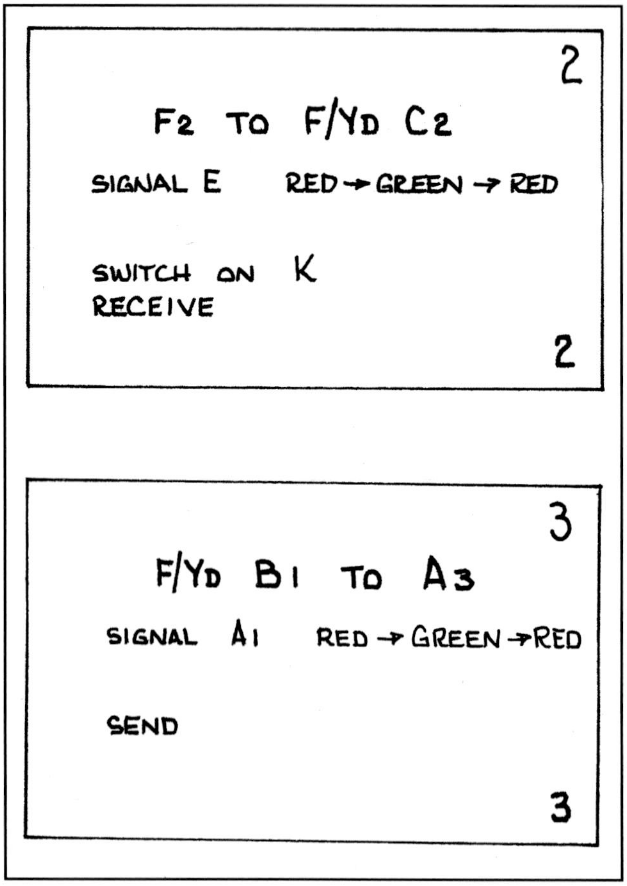

2
F2 TO F/YD C2
SIGNAL E RED → GREEN → RED
SWITCH ON K
RECEIVE
2
3
F/YD B1 TO A3
SIGNAL A1 RED → GREEN → RED
SEND
3

Left Examples of movement cards numbered in sequence, containing the minimum of necessary information.

Below The flip-over card-holder adapted from an old ring-binder.

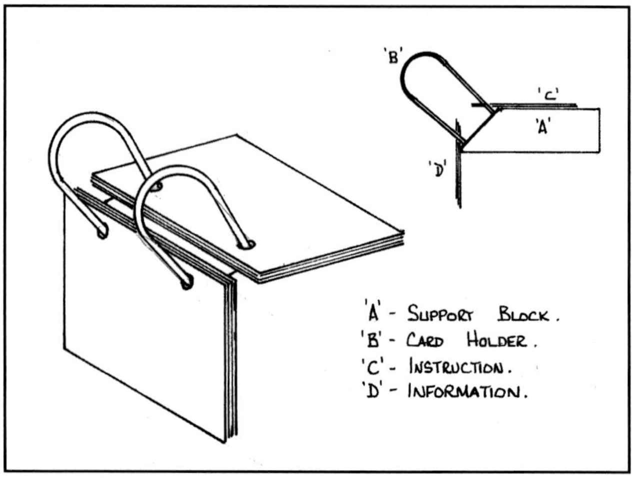

'B'
'C'
'A'
'D'
'A' - SUPPORT BLOCK.
'B' - CARD HOLDER.
'C' - INSTRUCTION.
'D' - INFORMATION.

Preparing for exhibitions

I have talked a lot about how small layouts can be easily exhibited, and this is true. However, it is only fair to point out that a lot of preparation is required. It is not just a matter of putting all you need in the back of the car and driving off! For the benefit of those who might be considering showing their layout, let me describe the process.

Invitations to exhibit your layout may come from someone asking you at an exhibition, or you may receive a letter or phone call, or your club secretary, having received an invitation for the club to be represented at an exhibition, may ask if you would be willing to do so.

The first stage, if you accept, is to make sure the Exhibition Manager has a copy of your hand-out giving the details he or she requires about your layout. More importantly, you must make sure that you have all the relevant information: date(s), location, opening and closing times, setting-up times, a map showing how to get to the venue, and agreed expenses (usually very helpful for both parties). It is important to enter the dates in you diary to avoid any possibility of double-booking, which will cause embarrassment all round.

Having accepted the invitation, you must make sure that your layout is working properly and is presentable; if the layout is stored it will be necessary to erect it just as it will be at the exhibition. I also have a little memo book in which I write all the jobs that need doing as they arise, or as I think of them; as they are done they are crossed off the list. This is also an idea I cribbed from Norman Eagles, of Sherwood fame!

Assuming that all the minor repair jobs have been done and the layout and its electrics are functioning properly, next turn your attention to the locos. Every one has to work properly if it is to run at the show. You have to be quite ruthless about this - any poor runners must be put on one side. The wheels of each loco have to be cleaned and pick-ups checked to ensure that, as far as possible, the loco will not let you down. Of course, from time to time a loco does go wrong at a show, but the risk of this must be kept to a minimum.

Having checked the layout and locos (and rolling-stock), now start thinking about loading the car in readiness for the journey, making sure that you don't leave anything vital behind. This is particularly relevant when you have to travel a long way to the show.

I have found that the only safe way to minimise the risk is to have an exhibition check-list. The day before I travel to an exhibition I get all the equipment together and check it off against the list, then I load the car on the day I travel (or sometimes on the night before if it is an early start); again, I have a routine for doing this. Finally, if an overnight stay is required, it is important not to forget your case!

You should also take spares - a controller, an AC transformer, plugs, switches and floodlights for the layout lighting, to name but a few items.

However, even with the best-laid plans things can go wrong, but there seems to be great camaraderie amongst exhibitors, and I have borrowed from others when I have forgotten something (an extension lead, for example) and have lent things to other exhibitors in a similar predicament.

6.
THE ULTIMATE

I suppose the ultimate aim for a railway modeller is to have a good layout in a room of its own. Not only must that room house the layout, but it must also have at least the basic facilities for a small workbench. I say 'basic facilities' because I think 'dirty jobs' like sawing wood should be done in the garage or outside, so that mess in the modelling room is kept to a minimum. It is also thus easier to justify having carpet on the floor, which not only makes the room more comfortable, but, if the room is upstairs, also has sound-deadening qualities.

The design and size of rooms in a modern house make a railway room difficult to accommodate unless you are prepared to extend the house, build a separate building in the garden or utilise the garage. I feel that the last two alternatives make your modelling habitat less comfortable; certainly you will need to ensure that the building or garage is properly heated, if nothing else. That said, I have used a shed for my railway modelling on two occasions because there was no other alternative, and it is possible to make such a building habitable. However, there is still the expense of buying the shed in the first place, fitting it out, and, worst of all in my opinion, the quick dash to the shed when it is pouring with rain!

Use of the garage for the layout is also popular with some people, and ingenious designs have been produced to allow the car to be accommodated as well, but I have to admit that it is not for me. Concrete floors are cold!

For all these reasons I would much prefer to have my layout in the house itself. There is another very good reason for this - security. Sadly we live in an age where burglary is common-place and an unattended building outside is very tempting to potential thieves or vandals.

I am very fortunate in being a vicar because vicarages usually have four bedrooms of a reasonable size. My sons have grown up, so our smallest bedroom was allocated as the Railway Room when we moved to our present home. My elder son, Justin, is a railway modeller too, and we are lucky that the loft is designed so that there is plenty of headroom. It had already been half boarded and a loft ladder fitted, so Justin installed carpets, lighting and his layout.

I have to admit that it is not perfect, not least because of the swings in temperature in the height of summer and the depth of winter, but if it was our own house we could do further work in the loft to make it more acceptable. Even so, with heating switched on in advance it is possible to work up there on all but the coldest days.

Many people have made their lofts very habitable and built excellent layouts, so if its design is such that the loft is a possibility, then go for it, because it is usually by far the largest space available in a house.

Unfortunately, modern house designs nearly always seem to incorporate W-trusses, which make the loft impossible to use, so modellers are forced to look elsewhere in the house. There have been all sorts of ingenious places found for layouts - under the stairs, over the stairwell, a hinged board in a bedroom, a layout around the walls of a room, in a cupboard, and so on. These have been described in more detail in Cyril Freezer's book *A Home For Your Railway*, published by Peco.

However, to return to the ultimate dream - the Railway Room. You will notice I said that the *smallest* bedroom in our vicarage was allocated as the Railway Room. It measures 9 ft 10 in by 7 ft 6 in, so had I been building a large layout it would have been impossible to accommodate it. Then I would have been vying for space in the loft with Justin, looking at a shed again or perhaps building a portable layout that could be stored in a small bedroom or in the garage. Thus building small layouts makes it easier, I believe, to achieve the ultimate dream in a modern house.

What goes into this Railway Room? First of all the layout, second a small workbench, and third all the stock, unmade kits, paints, brushes, etc. Clearly, therefore, storage is of crucial importance. I strongly advise against supporting the layout on legs and using the space underneath for unorganised storage, because in no time you will have a mess and never be able to find a thing. Stock, etc, could be accommodated there in a *tidy* manner, and maybe the workbench could be fitted with castors so that it too could be stored away when not in use.

In this connection the best thing that happened to me was when in the early 1980s - before I was ordained - we had new kitchen units fitted. I recognised the old ones as valuable storage space and stopped the builder from throwing them out. Instead they were put in the modelling room, which was then a small room we had made by extending the garage and partitioning it off. The builder said he was fitting another kitchen down the road and asked if I wanted those units too, and I eagerly agreed.

Those kitchen units have gone with us every time we have moved since, and they are worth their weight in gold. I have more than I need, but the surplus ones go in the garage for storage of gardening materials and so on. I removed the worktops and, of course, the sink unit and replaced them with half-inch chipboard to ensure they were all the same height. However, I did not throw away the worktops, as they were used for making benches. Justin used one for his in the loft, and I used one for the same purpose in a garage.

You can often find that other furniture outlives its usefulness in the house but is ideal for the modelling room. When Justin was a baby we bought a whitewood chest of drawers for the nursery and suitably painted it. When he grew up he wanted different furniture, so the chest was quickly commandeered for model railway storage.

Likewise, when Justin and Paul were into computers, we bought a self-assembly computer desk. When Paul left home the desk became redundant, and we were on the

verge of selling it when I suddenly realised that it had the makings of a very good small workbench. So that too was quickly grabbed for the modelling room.

I covered the whole of the larger horizontal surface with a piece of laminate cut to size and stuck on with impact adhesive, then fitted a vice and a four-way extension socket into which is permanently plugged the bench light, and other electrical items (eg soldering iron, controller) when required. On the smaller horizontal surface, where the screen would normally go, I put storage racks and some track (one length of O gauge and one of OO) to be used as short test tracks. Finally, an A4-size cutting mat was affixed.

The space between the upper and lower horizontal surfaces is used for storage. Of the two smaller compartments, one holds a small electric drill and the associated tools, while the other holds a box in which parts of uncompleted kits can be safely kept. The large space between the two smaller compartments is used for tool storage. I made two pull-out trays, divided into sections, in which I keep the small tools that one normally uses for modelling. Larger tools are kept in my toolbox, which stands on the old whitewood chest of drawers.

I am very proud of the toolbox. It was made by my father in the late 1920s when he was an apprentice fitter and turner at the GWR Works at Swindon. It followed him to Pressed Steel Co in Oxford in 1938, and when he became a foreman in 1945 he brought it home and there it stayed until he gave it to me in 1986. It is now nearly 70 years old and is a real link with the GWR of the past. Perhaps the fact that my father and both my grandfathers worked at Swindon

The work area in my Railway Room, showing the converted computer desk and other furniture mentioned in the text.

made it inevitable that I should become interested in railways and model railways at a very early age.

The final piece of furniture in my Railway Room is a single wardrobe in which I store all my stock boxes.

This is the first time in 45 years of modelling that I have been able to have *sole* use of a room in the house, and it has been worth waiting for. It means that I can go in there any time I have a few minutes or longer to spare, and I can leave uncompleted kits on the bench and return to them later. All this brings with it a responsibility, of course - I must keep it clean! Therefore I always clean up the bench when I have finished work, and if I have made a mess on the floor, through drilling or filing, I make sure I pop downstairs to get the vacuum cleaner. In this way the room is kept tidy and clean and, if someone goes in to get something or pull the curtains, they do not pick up the mess on their shoes and transfer it to the rest of the house. I think this is very important!

I currently have two layouts. One is stored on top of a kitchen unit in the garage with its own protective wooden cover. The layout is only 3 ft 9 in by 1 ft 10 in and does not take up much room at all. The other is 9 ft 6 in long and is under construction in the Railway Room.

One further tip. I always keep a notebook in the Railway Room for each layout, recording in them jobs that need to be done. In the case of a completed layout, the job may have come to light in an operating session or at an exhibition. It may be that a certain loco needs attention because it did not run properly, or a repair needs to be done to the layout itself. In the case of a layout under construction, the jobs may be ones that I have already planned and are simply listed to ensure that I do not forget them, or it may be that I list down alternative ways of doing things as I think of them. Whatever the reason, as the job is done it is crossed off.

Finally, on the question of storage, do not forget stock boxes. These are vital if your stock is to be kept and transported safely. When I was in the Oxford MRC in the late 1960s, John Peverel-Cooper designed a stock box that became the norm in the club, and was the subject of an article in the *Railway Modeller* at the time. I still have one that dates from that time, but as it was for OO rolling-stock, I passed it on to Justin some years ago. It is still going strong, although he did have to replace the foam in it recently - but that was after 30 years!

When I moved to 7 mm narrow gauge, I built my own stock boxes to a different design. Instead of a hinged lid I used a sliding lid, which is simply a piece of hardboard. The compartments are lined with foam for obvious reasons. By a coincidence, these same stock boxes can be used for 7 mm standard gauge wagons too - usually of the open variety - and this I have done.

Earlier I warned against letting good storage units be discarded. The same applies to boxes, etc, that can be used for stock storage. My current 7 mm standard gauge locomotives are stored in a variety of containers. The Lima Class 33s and two Lima 4Fs are stored in two drawers in which I used to keep odds and ends. It transpired that they were exactly the right height and length for the storage of O gauge locos (standing on their wheels), so I fitted dividers to allow me to store four locos in each box. Again, each compartment is lined with foam. The lid is screwed on at the moment, although it is intended to fit hinges at a later date.

Another loco storage box is made from an old picnic box that was surplus to requirements, again divided into compartments and lined with foam. Another example is a small suitcase; the locos are carried in boxes which fit tightly inside it, again using foam to protect the stock.

Justin bought a CD storage rack for his room and the cardboard box in

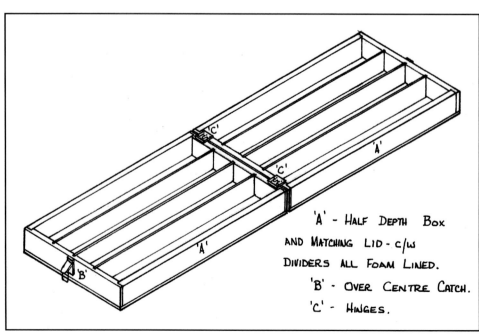

'A' - HALF DEPTH BOX AND MATCHING LID - c/w DIVIDERS ALL FOAM LINED.

'B' - OVER CENTRE CATCH.

'C' - HINGES.

The stock box designed by John Peverel-Cooper.

which it came was quite substantial. I measured the inside of the box, then took a cutting list to a DIY store where they cut me the necessary pieces of hardboard with which to line the box and make dividers. These slide in between pieces of quarter-inch square wood glued to the sides. The locomotives are stored across the width of the box, and this time the protection is afforded by plastic 'bubble sheets' that line the compartments. All these stock boxes are stored in the above-mentioned wardrobe, and have been made at very little cost.

I appreciate that not everybody will be able to aspire to the ultimate of having a dedicated Railway Room in the house, but if you are able it is worth planning in some detail to get the best out of it. If no room is available, don't despair! I understand that P. D. Hancock's famous Craig & Mertonford Railway was built around the walls of his bedroom in a flat in Edinburgh, and if I could build a layout to that standard, I would be highly delighted.

Wherever you keep your layout, the most important thing is that you work on it, build your rolling-stock, are happy with it and enjoy your modelling. Utopia can wait!

Right The stock box built into the CD rack cardboard box.

Below A stock box with a sliding lid.

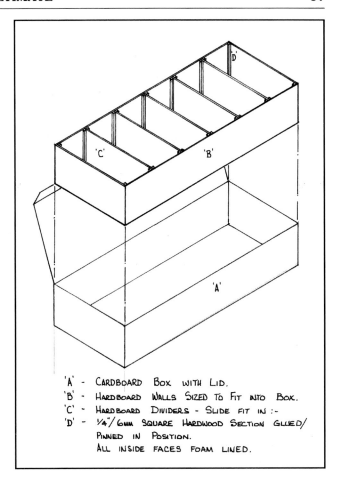

'A' - CARDBOARD BOX WITH LID.
'B' - HARDBOARD WALLS SIZED TO FIT INTO BOX.
'C' - HARDBOARD DIVIDERS - SLIDE FIT IN :-
'D' - ¼"/6MM SQUARE HARDWOOD SECTION GLUED/ PINNED IN POSITION.
ALL INSIDE FACES FOAM LINED.

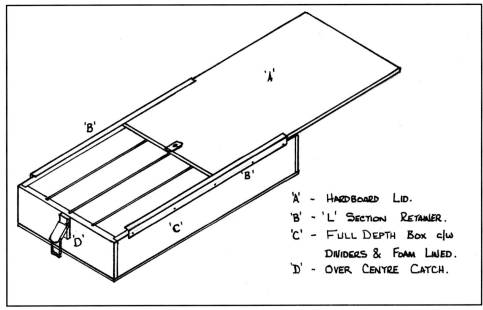

'A' - HARDBOARD LID.
'B' - 'L' SECTION RETAINER.
'C' - FULL DEPTH BOX c/w DIVIDERS & FOAM LINED.
'D' - OVER CENTRE CATCH.

7.
SMALL LAYOUTS GALLERY

This section of the book describes a number of small layouts of various gauges and sizes, representing actual examples of what I have been talking about up to this point. The majority are layouts that I have built myself, and two that I built with Justin and Paul. Then follow a number of layouts built by other people who have been kind enough to write about them for this book. The friendship and co-operation of fellow railway modellers is something I have valued very much over the years, and these contributions so willingly provided are a very tangible sign of this, and for which I am very grateful. The last layout is one built by Justin.

South Muxton branch

This is a description at my first serious attempt at railway modelling in 1966, after a few years of 'pipe-dreaming' and planning. The layout was built on two permanent baseboards that together measured 9 by 2 feet, and there was a portable fiddle yard that measured 6 by 1 feet.

The planning for the layout was started in January 1966 when I knew that we would be moving from a flat to a new house. My wife, who is very interested in railway modelling, had agreed that I could build a layout along one wall of the dining room. I armed myself with some squared paper and drawing instruments and started drawing various plans to fit into the space available. One of the big advantages of a layout in such a location is the availability of storage space under the baseboard, but more of this later.

Various plans were drawn up and put aside, and after studying them all I eventually decided on the plan shown here. The name of the layout was a combination of the name of the village in which we lived (Southmoor) and my wife's home (Muxton), which is in Shropshire.

The plan had to satisfy my requirement for a busy terminus because during the two years we lived in the flat I had been acquiring Hornby locomotives and building rolling-stock. I had quite a few small locomotives, so I

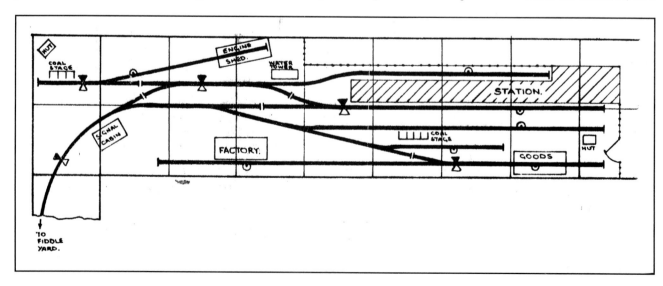

Below left and right Plan and view of my South Muxton layout. All the buildings were Superquick or Bilteezi. *Plan M. Gee/Photo R. Edmiston*

dispensed with a crossover from the platform road to the adjoining road, removing all the trains with the station pilot (except of course the diesel set and the auto-coach). It also saved two points!

Baseboards and track

I was fortunate in having a friend who was a carpenter by trade, and he made the baseboards for me. They were made of insulation board on a framework of 2 by 1 inch timber. The two main baseboards were made first and I drew the layout plan on them at full size. At this stage 2 by 2 inch legs were fitted and the track-laying commenced.

I used Peco Streamline track and points, and after much thought decided to use balsa wood for the trackbed. This was rather expensive, but it had the advantage that it could be easily cut with a craft knife, and a nice sloping shoulder could be obtained using a Surform. The trackbed was cut out and held in position with panel pins, then it was all painted grey; I have never used this method since. The track was then pinned to the trackbed using Peco pins.

The next step was to ballast the track with Peco ballast. A runny solution of Casco glue was made up and dropped between the sleepers with a small paintbrush, and also brushed on the trackbed shoulders. The ballast was then sprinkled on liberally and allowed to dry, the surplus being removed for re-use. This may seem a laborious way of laying and ballasting track, but it had three distinct advantages. The first was that time could be taken to lay the track properly rather than the messy business of laying it on to an already-glued trackbed, when it can be a race against time before the glue dries. Second, if ever I had wanted to alter the track layout I could easily have moved the track and the bases. Third, the ballast came level with the sleepers. Furthermore, once you become used to dropping the glue between the sleepers, it is surprising how quickly it can be done. The ballast was then sealed in with a weak solution of Polycell, another method that I no longer use.

Electrical control

I had already decided that I would use a diagrammatic control panel and H&M point motors worked by the 'electric pencil' system. I had a piece of plywood about the right size so I painted it white and drew out the track diagram on it in red. I approached the drawing of the circuit diagram with some trepidation because I had always considered myself to be ignorant of even the simplest electrical matters, but it had to be done and I found that by taking it step by step, it was not nearly as difficult as I had imagined. In many magazine articles on layouts the electrical side is often dismissed in a few words and this, I feel, increases a beginner's impression that it is difficult. Therefore, in an endeavour to correct this impression, diagrams are shown overleaf.

The first shows the control panel. Brass strip was screwed to the back of the panel and wires attached as shown. It is important to make a decision at the start as to which rail will be the 'switch' rail, the other being the 'strip' rail; this is easily seen in the diagram. Dead sections were wired as normal.

The control panel was screwed to the inside of the front baseboard frame after all possible work that could be done away from the baseboard had been completed. The wires for the feeds and section breaks were soldered to the rails, then it was a simple job to sit beneath the baseboard on a small folding stool and make the necessary connections.

The electric pencil method of point operation is shown in the second diagram. It was simplicity itself to install and operate. Brass screws were inserted right through the control panel (two for each set of points),

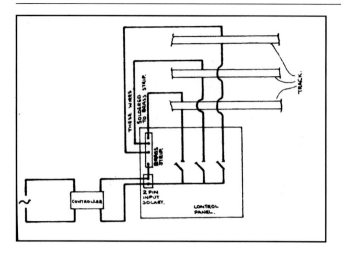

Track switches wired from the control panel. M. Gee

leaving their heads on the painted line. The electric pencil (which can be a pointed metal rod or jack-plug on the end of a thick wire) was attached directly to one terminal of the 16V AC supply. The backs of the screws were wired to the point in question, each to the appropriate terminal. A touch of the 'pencil' on either screw head completed the circuit and moved the points. All the points in the fiddle yard were hand operated.

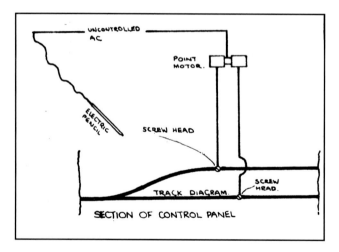

Using the 'electric pencil' method of point control. M. Gee

Scenery
The buildings were a mixture of Airfix, Superquick and Bilteezi, made by both my wife Celia and myself. The backscenes were all made by Celia and were a mixture of Hamblings and Peco backscenes that she cut out and altered, then stuck on to hardboard to make what I consider was a very convincing view.

Storage
I installed shelves under the layout and stored the fiddle yard board beneath it as well. Some shelves were

used for my modelling requirements (eg stock storage, tools and unfinished kits), the remainder being used by Celia for storing sewing and knitting. The shelves were easily made from hardboard braced with 2 by 1 inch timber, and they fitted on to supports screwed to the legs from front to back. The fiddle yard board rested on two similar supports. The front and side of the boards were covered with curtains.

This method enabled me to keep all my modelling requirements in one place, and Celia was happy because she had additional storage space, which is at a premium in modern houses. When the layout was operated the fiddle yard board was supported at one end by a small trestle that rested on the dining table and, at the other end by a hinged leg and a coach bolt that joined it to the main board. The tracks were joined by a separate insert.

Pen-y-Bord

This was a minimum space HOn9 scale layout, which I built in 1968 to assess the gauge before I embarked on anything more ambitious, as well as to please Celia, who always liked the little HOn9 scale loco-motives and rolling-stock.

Celia decided that she must have a new ironing board, but when she took the covers off the old one - destined for the refuse collection - she noticed that it was made of a 'baseboard type of wood'. Being practical she put it in the garage for my attention. It was small, but it was of course self-supporting, so I needed little more encouragement, and after a quick measuring session, I started to draw up possible plans, culminating in the one shown in the diagram.

The board measured 3 ft 5 in by 1 ft, and although the surface was not suitable as a baseboard, a covering of Sundeala offcuts soon rectified that problem. Apart from being a trial run in HOn9 gauge, the other object of the layout was to test its capabilities for exhibitions, and from that point of view it was admirable. It was small, compact, easily transportable and simple to erect and take down. The stock was carried in a box measuring 8 by 6 by 3 inches, so the whole lot was easily carried in a car.

As can be seen from the diagram opposite, the lay-out had a hidden storage siding, a continuous circuit, a reversing loop and a terminal station. It used only four points.

Trackwork
I use Peco Crazy-track and points, with my normal practice of ballasting after the track had been laid. The amount of ballasting necessary was relatively small, the hidden sections not being treated. The

Right Plan of Pen-y-Bord.
M. *Gee*

Below right A very much
younger author pictured in
1968 with the complete ironing board layout. The standard folding legs are clearly
shown. *Oxford Mail & Times*

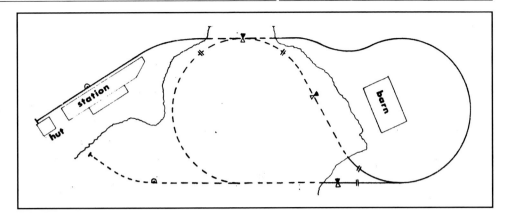

Right Plan of Pen-y-Bord. M. *Gee*

points were operated
manually; the two at the
rear of the layout were
easily accessible, while
the two under the hill
were operated by ⅟₁₆ inch
diameter wire, using a
straight push-pull action.

Electrical control

This was simple as there
were only two feed points
and three section switch-
es, plus the separate feed
via a DPDT switch for
the reversing loop. The
wiring was entirely con-
ventional and followed
the usual textbook meth-
ods. The current was con-
nected to the layout by a
two-pin plug and socket.
The plug came direct
from an H&M Minipack
controller to the socket,
which was hidden under
an Airfix hut near the

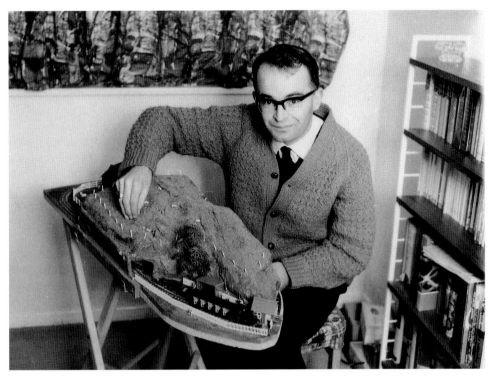

station. The roof of the hut was only lightly glued, in
case access to the socket was necessary.

Scenery and rolling-stock

A great part of the layout was covered by a hill, which
was made from Mod-roc laid over screwed-up damp
newspaper. When it had set hard, the newspaper was
removed, leaving a hollow hill. The Mod-roc was
painted with Humbrol track colour and covered,
while the paint was still wet, with Dee-Ess scenic
material. Some grey paint was also used to simulate
rocks. Slaters fence-posts and fishing line were used to
make the fence that surrounded the hill, and a box of
Merit sheep and a shepherd made up the layout's pop-
ulation.

At one end of the board, at 'ground' level, was the
station, which was made from balsa wood. The hut
and platform supports were covered with stone paper,

while the platform itself was covered with black Dee-
Ess material to simulate a cindered surface. The whole
area was surrounded by Airfix station fencing and the
ground was covered with the same material as the
hill, the method of application being the same. The
station was finished off with a tree and the hut
already mentioned.

I was at a loss to know what to do with the other
end. I wanted a large building that would hide the
entrance to the reversing loop, mask the end view of
the switches and wiring and the handling and stock
movement that would go on under the hill. After one
or two false starts I purchased a Superquick barn, one
of the few buildings that was tall enough for my pur-
poses, but still in keeping with the surroundings. It
was meant to be part of a larger farm that had been
severed by the railway line. However, it was connected by a cinder path that passed over the railway track

through a gate in the Airfix lineside fencing. The board in this area was covered in green flock, with black material to represent the cinders where necessary. It was populated by four cows and some farmworkers, all from the Merit range.

The stock used on the layout was standard Playcraft and Eggerbahn.

Storage

For storage and transport I built a hardboard 'coffin' that fitted over the layout. It kept out the dust when stored and prevented any damage and accidental knocks during transit to and from exhibitions.

Draycott Valley Railway

Baseboard and trackwork

This layout was built in early 1969. The baseboard was made in the conventional manner, using 2 by 1 inch timber and half-inch Sundeala board. The trackwork was all Peco; it was ballasted with a mixture of Eames and Peco ballast and painted with Humbrol Track Colour paint. The track plan was drawn direct on to the baseboard using a straight edge and a crude compass, which consisted of a piece of wood with a pivot hole drilled into it and more holes at the required radii. A nail was driven lightly through the pivot hole and a pencil inserted at the required radius and, using the nail as a pivot, the line was drawn.

Draycott Valley Railway.

The track was pinned at about every seventh sleeper with Peco track pins on the outside of the sleepers (two per sleeper). The ballast was applied after the track was laid; a weak mixture of Casco glue was applied between the sleepers and the loose ballast added and pressed down. When dry, the surplus was removed.

The two points on public view were electrically operated by Peco motors mounted on adaptor bases, which were hidden under huts. The remaining points were on the hidden part of the layout and were hand-operated.

Electrical control

The layout was wired in the conventional manner, with three feeds and five dead sections. The control panel was portable and was home-made using an old Trix transformer and Codar modules mounted on an old portable wireless case. Connection to the layout was simple via two plugs and sockets, one for AC and one for DC. On/off switches were mounted on the board.

Scenery

I think it would have been impossible to model realistic narrow gauge line scenery accurately in a space of 4 by 2 feet, so I aimed at creating an overall impression; judging by the comments received at the 1969 National Model Railway Hobby Show, I was reasonably successful. The main part of the scenery was made from polystyrene off-cuts, which were easily cut and carved; it was also extremely light. After being stuck to the baseboard it was painted dark grey. Celia, being much more of a scenic expert than me, lent a

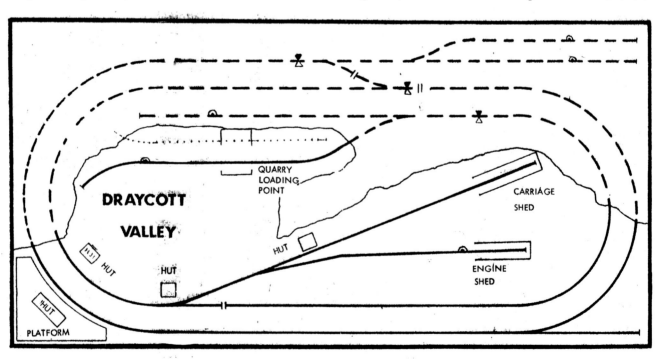

A photo of the tipper dock on the Draycott Valley Railway. The polystyrene backscene, painted grey, shows up well.
R. Edmiston

hand in applying the lichen and scenic material. The engine shed was Playcraft, two huts were made from Superquick signal box kits, and the remaining hut was Airfix. The coach shed, the quarry unloading stage and the station buildings were simply made using balsa wood, Superquick stone papers and Slaters corrugated iron. The layout was peopled by Merit figures.

Many people ask how long a layout has taken to build. I kept a record on this one, which shows that our hobby need not be too time-consuming. It took approximately 70 hours to build, spread over seven weeks, which gives an average of 10 hours per week of weekend and evening spare time.

Rolling-stock

The rolling-stock consisted of four Minitrains diesels, two Eggerbahn works locomotives, one Playcraft locomotive, three Eggerbahn short coaches, one Playcraft 'toast-rack' coach and ten assorted Minitrains wagons.

The locomotives were all numbered by sticking Slaters numbers on the sides of the cabs; these covered the existing ones if carefully applied. The layout was operated to a sequence timetable, which portrayed the typical day's workings on this imaginary line.

009 MPD

Baseboard and trackwork

I built this 009 layout in 1972. The main baseboard only measured 35 by 21 inches, with a fiddle yard measuring 22 by 9 inches, but I thoroughly enjoyed building it and operating it at exhibitions. The inspiration came from a fellow member of the Oxford MRC who some time previously had built a layout of an MPD in 00 gauge, which I thought was marvellous and wanted to do something similar in the smaller scale.

The baseboard was chipboard with a minimal 2 by 1 inch framing, and the track was laid directly on to it; the track design was very simple, as shown in the plan. The track was set in Alabastine, and the whole baseboard, except inside the engine shed, was covered in the same material. This was then painted with a mixture of black Humbrol paint and thinners.

The fiddle yard was connected to the main board by two brass flap-back hinges with pins slight turned down for easy removal. The layout rested on the base of an old kitchen table with detachable legs, and the fiddle yard was supported at the end by a 2 by 1 inch leg, which was screwed on. For transport to exhibitions the table base, the legs, the main board, the fiddle yard and boxes of stock easily fitted into the car, together with the usual tool box, spare controller, etc.

Scenery

The scenery, although basically proprietary kits suitably modified, looked effective and many complimentary remarks were made on this aspect at exhibitions.

The buildings consisted mainly of Airfix engine shed parts. I used four of these kits, all of which had the lower four courses of brickwork cut away to make a more suitable overall height for 009 models. The water tank on the shed was the top half of a Superquick water tower mounted on a piece of Plasticard. This material was also used where it was not possible to use the Airfix parts, and for this reason all the roof of the building was covered with

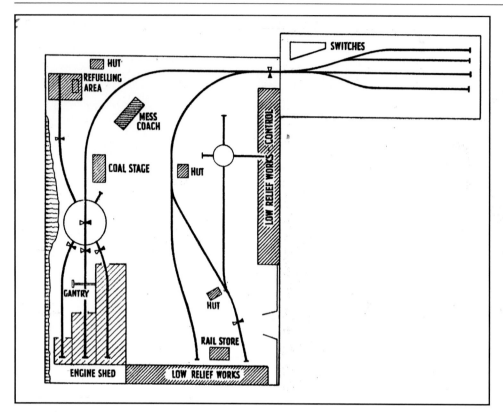

Left Plan of the MPD in 009.

Below left An overall view of my narrow gauge MPD and Works in 009. The fiddle yard was connected at the top left-hand corner by brass flap-back hinges. *Allan Wood*

of place and certainly made a world of difference to the scenic side, bringing the whole place to life.

The embankment at the front of the layout was made from Polystyrene blocks stuck down and carved to shape with a hot Oryx soldering iron. After a wash of thin Alabastine, it was painted with green gloss paint and, while still wet, sprinkled with scenic compound and allowed to dry. The fence was constructed from Slaters fence-posts and fishing line; a laborious job, but worth the effect, for it gave the characteristic sag of old wire fencing. The backscene was hand-painted by Bill Simpson, then a fellow member of Oxford MRC, and was also very effective.

Superquick tile paper. The sides were painted with Humbrol red and, when dry, the whole structure was given a wash of black paint and thinners, which gave a surprisingly effective grubby effect.

The refuelling area for the diesels was an Airfix garage kit roof supported on dowelling, and underneath was a body from an old Trix tank wagon. The lifting gantry was basically made from an Airfix signal gantry kit plus some Balsa wood; the latter was being used for the coaling stage. The mess coach was an old Lilliput vehicle, which was 'dirtied' with black paint and thinners. The turntable was made from wood with parts from an old Airfix turntable kit for the sides, and was operated by the usual arrangement of Meccano parts and a hand-turned crank. I added over 100 Airfix figures to the layout; they did not look out

Electrical control

The electrical side of the layout was also simple. The three points were electrically operated by point motors hidden by items of scenery and energised by the 'electric pencil' system, which worked very well. I wanted all the switches and controls on the main baseboard, which is an aid to portability and saves a lot of time making the various connections. However, in the end I could not fit the controller to the board for lack of space, but all the switches were fitted. The Codar controller was set in a piece of hardboard, which was screwed to the baseboard with two screws.

To start operations all I had to do was connect a plug to the socket to energise the track; put two wires from the Codar unit to an H&M Safety Minor (AC output); plug in the mains; and everything was ready to go.

A close-up of a loco on the turntable. The loco is a cut-down Airfix 'Pug' and the turntable sides are made from the Airfix turntable kit. *Brian Higgins*

Operation

At exhibitions a sequence timetable was followed and the fiddle yard was equipped with shelves on which the spare stock and small tools (screwdrivers, small pliers, etc) were kept to obviate the continual diving into the stock and tool box. This was very useful and something I have repeated on other layouts.

It gave me great pleasure when the layout received the trophy for the best layout for attention to scenic detail at the 1973 Oxford Exhibition.

Narrow gauge loco shed

My main interests in modelling are building model locomotives and layouts. However, if you have a lot of locos they either need a large layout on which to run them, or they do not get run very often. My narrow gauge loco depot was small but the very nature of it meant that it accommodated 26 locos in the sequence of operations used at exhibitions.

Baseboards and trackwork

The depot was built on two baseboards, each measuring 40 by 14 inches. In one sense it had a 'gimmick' in that it had no points at all, and the main feature was the movement of locos in and out of the depot. The hidden sidings were on a pivoted sector plate.

The baseboards were made for me by a carpenter friend and consisted of a glued and screwed 2 by 1 inch framework to which was screwed half-inch chipboard. The boards were held together by 1 inch square flap-back hinges, which gave reasonable alignment of the tracks. Once erected, the boards were firmly clamped in position by two G-clamps to ensure that they did not move. For storage and transport the boards were held face to face by bolting them to a piece of chipboard at each end. In fact, to make life even easier I fitted four castors to the underside of the bottom board so that, once out of the car, the layout could be pushed into the exhibition hall rather than carried!

I used Peco 0-16.5 track and, as can be seen from the track plan, it was simplicity itself. The most

Plan of the 0-16.5 narrow gauge depot.

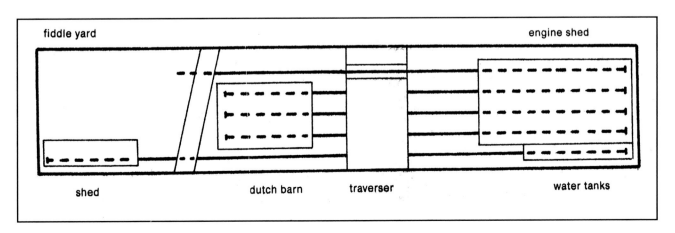

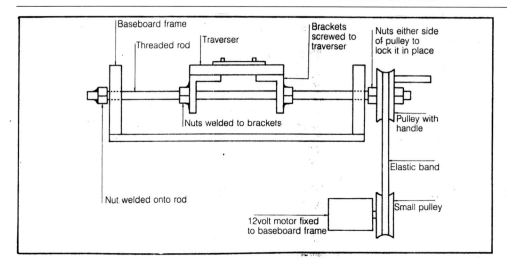

Sketch of the traverser and its operating mechanism. See also the photograph on page 83.

important aspect was to ensure that the parallel roads on each side of the traverser lined up with the traverser when in position.

The traverser itself ran on a ⅜ inch diameter threaded rod, which had a nut welded on to it at one end and a pulley fitted between two nuts at the other end. The traverser was simply a piece of wood and it was fixed to the rod by an inverted 'U' consisting of two L-shaped brackets. Each bracket had a nut welded to it and the threaded rod ran through the nuts. When the rod was turned the traverser moved backed and forth.

The pulley had a handle fitted to it so that it could be moved by hand, but the usual method of movement was by an elastic band connected to a pulley glued to the shaft of an electric motor. The system may sound crude

but it was certainly very effective and proved itself at long exhibitions. All that was needed was a few reserve elastic bands!

From an operating point of view it really was satisfying to set the controller so that the traverser ran across the width of the layout at a very slow speed. It also gave you a chance for a breather, and it certainly seemed to hold the viewing public spellbound.

Scenery

The visible track was covered with Polyfilla to which had been added dark-coloured powder paints to give it a base colour. When this set the grass (dyed medical lint), the rock-face backscene (Ossett Mouldings) and the buildings were added.

The main building was made for me by a friend and it looked very effective. Basically it was made from hardboard covered in scribed modelling compound. I made the 'dutch barn' from Plasticard, and sandpaper was used for the roof. The coach shed, which hid the fiddle yard, was also made from Plasticard, and Slaters corrugated sheets were used for the roof.

Various other details were added, such as Airfix water towers mounted on a balsa wood framework and a lifting gantry made from pieces of an Airfix signal gantry kit, and a Brittains stone wall was fixed all the way along both boards.

A close-up of the locos on the shed on my narrow gauge loco depot layout, which was exhibited at a number of shows including the 1981 Model Railway Club Exhibition at Central Hall. The 'dutch barn'-type shed was made from Plasticard with individual rows of tiles cut down from fine-grade sandpaper stuck on to it. *Joe Prestidge*

Above Another view of the 'dutch barn' structure showing the roof in more detail. It also shows how the strips lifted in time; for that reason it's not a method I would use again. *Joe Prestidge*

Right The inside of the engine shed. I spent a happy hour or two making the bench and putting the various tools on it. Note also the bricked-up windows - another easy thing to model. When the roof was on not much of this was visible, but I knew it was there! *Barry Poultney*

Then the addition of the detail really started. A workbench was installed just inside the main shed (complete with shelves), together with tools and workpeople, trolleys, lamps, rubbish, loco wheels, sacks, fire irons, oil drums, and all the small detail that I think is essential for a layout of this size if it is to be interesting to the public at shows.

Electrical control

The wiring of the track was simple. Each track had its own feed and one or two dead sections depending on whether it was in the main shed (in which case it had two) or under the 'dutch barn' (only one).

An ECM controller (centre off) was used. It was mounted in a small box that rested on a shelf at the back of the layout and was fed by an ECM transformer, which was on the floor at exhibitions.

The main control panel was screwed to the back of the main board behind the engine shed. The switches were laid out in rows with the relevant dead section push-button switches (push to make) under each feed

switch. Also on the control panel were separate switches for the traverser motor and feed, the two colour light signals and the light in the fiddle yard control panel, which indicated to the operator there whether he was to send or receive a loco, or neither.

The fiddle yard had three roads each fed from a rotary switch and each having a dead section operated by a push-button switch.

The main shed had interior lights, which were operated from an H&M controller; they could be turned on or off, bright or dim, as required.

The current to the traverser track was picked up by a piece of brass shim glued to each end of the traverser, which rubbed on a length of OO gauge track fixed on each side of the well.

The Shed

This layout was built in 1985 and followed a similar format to the layout just described, except that I used a turntable instead of a traverser and it was on one board instead of two, thus making transport and setting up for exhibitions even easier.

Baseboard and trackwork

This measured 66 by 22 inches and was 12 mm thick on 3 by 1 inch framing; this deeper framing gave added strength and better protection for the under-baseboard wiring, etc. The baseboard stood on two trestles at exhibitions. I was fortunate in being able to have the turntable well cut for me at work, thus ensuring that it was perfectly circular.

The trackwork was all Peco, and before it was laid the plan was drawn out full size on shelf paper and also on the baseboard itself; some minor alterations were made at this stage. All section breaks were cut after the track was laid using a mini electric drill and a cutting disc.

The 'ballast' was a mixture of Polyfilla and black and white powder paint, giving a dark grey gelatinous mess that was trowelled between the running rails and over the sleepers to give the appearance of a typical MPD area. It is better to mix the powder paint with the Polyfilla rather than paint the Polyfilla afterwards, which avoids any white showing through if the surface is chipped. The Polyfilla was left to set hard and any surplus, which adversely affected good running by sticking to the inside of the rails, was scraped away. The tops of the rails were also kept polished to ensure good electrical contact.

Scenery

The engine shed and all the low-relief buildings were salvaged from previous layouts. The former was made

for me by a friend from hardboard and Das modelling compound, and the roofs were removable for access. The low-relief buildings were made from Plasticard stuck to a hardboard or Sundeala frame.

On such a small layout I felt that to add atmosphere there should be many people, small huts, tools and suchlike.

Probably one of the most satisfying jobs was the building of the fence all along the front of the layout. This had a stripwood frame to which I stuck individual planks made from some old fibre sleepers I had had for ages. To add effect, in some cases the planks were sloped, some were left out, and corrugated sheet was used to repair damaged planks. All this combined to give the impression of a 'tatty' fence such as one often sees near railways. There was also a gang putting in new fence-posts and gates. The fence also had some topical graffiti scrawled on it, as had one of the water towers.

The diesel fuelling point was on the main entry track just before the turntable, and was a tank from an Airfix tanker kit mounted on 0-16.5 sleepers in a similar way to the water tank on the Ffestiniog Railway at Tan-y-Bwlch. The coaling stage was made from half of a Japanese bridge kit in 1:35 scale to which a sleeper fence was added, made from scribed balsa wood. The lifting gantry in front of the water towers was again made from cut-down Airfix signal gantry parts.

As with the previous layout, inside the engine shed there was a bench, and I spent a happy couple of hours making drawers. Unfortunately when the roof was on it was not visible, but I knew it was there, and the addition of lights inside the engine shed improved the chances of it being seen by the viewing public.

The turntable worked through a Meccano worm and gearwheel using a universal joint. It was powered by a 12V electric motor, operated through the controller, and the drive was by elastic band. I found this simple and effective.

The shed building had been previously used on my narrow gauge MPD layout, which only goes to show that, if you break up a layout, you should do so with care and salvage as much as you can for future use. *Barry Poultney*

Another view of the layout showing the dilapidated fence with the 'drunken' planks and pieces of metal where the planks have gone. Note also the gantry made from Airfix signal gantry parts. *Barry Poultney*

Electrical control

The wiring was completed before the ballast was laid to ensure that the locos would run on all sections of the track. The nature of the layout meant that there were as many as eight track feeds and 30 dead sections, plus separate feeds for the sector plate, turntable track and turntable motor. All this was planned in advance with the help of my elder son, Justin. It may sound complicated, but if it is done logically it is not difficult.

I decided I wanted the very minimum of wires going into the baseboard, so the control panel was an integral part of it. There were only four plugs to connect - two for the AC supply and two for the wheel-cleaning brush.

The track feeds were fed through a rotary switch and there was a separate switch for the sector plate. A DPDT (double-pole double-throw) switch for the turntable powered either the motor or the track; this avoided the possibility of a loco on the turntable moving while being turned.

An ECM Compspeed controller was built into the panel, but provision was made for a hand-held AMR to be plugged in through a five-pin DIN plug.

The dead sections were wired directly to a bank of three switch panels, each containing six DPDT switches; by using 15 of these, all 30 dead sections were covered and there were three spare. The use of the rotary switch for the track meant that only one track could be energised at a time, thus ensuring that locos could not move on more than one. Also on the panel were the switches for one two-aspect colour light signal, and the lights in the yard. The lights in the engine shed were controlled through a dimmer switch.

The AC current was provided by an ECM transformer and the yard lights, the red and green mimic signal lights in the panel and the interior shed lights were powered by a small cheap Mainline three-position controller built into the baseboard.

It was not difficult to operate the layout as there was a track plan screwed to the back of the backscene with all the sections and feeds numbered.

Operation

I firmly believe that, particulary at exhibitions, aimless movements on a layout become boring for the operator as well as for the public, who have paid to come in. Therefore as already mentioned I always operate my layouts to a sequence that is written out on cards. Not only does this ensure that the operator does not get bored, it also means that, if asked questions by the public, he knows from where to carry on. It also allows the operators to change over with a minimum of disruption.

Brynglas

Being a volunteer guard on the Talyllyn Railway, I was attracted to the track plan at Brynglas, which is one of the passing loops on the line. I also wanted, as usual, to make the layout easily transportable to exhibitions, so I started planning and the outcome is shown in the plan overleaf. Those that know the Talyllyn Railway will see that it is not a prototypical model of Brynglas, but as the inspiration came from there, that is the name I gave it.

Baseboards and trackwork

As seems to be quite usual for me, I started the wrong way round! I had a piece of Sundeala board left over from an extension we had built to our house, so I bought a Peco 0-16.5 'Y' point and two lengths of

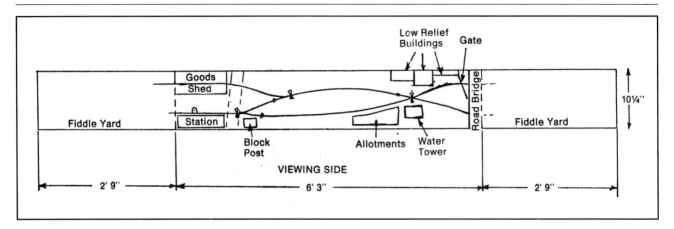

Top Plan of the Brynglas layout.

Middle An overall view of the station end of Brynglas, show-ing the station building, the goods shed, the block post and var-ious items of detail. The Peco backscene blends in quite well.
Barry Poultney

Bottom A train in the loop. Note the electrically operated uncoupling ramps and the two white-painted sleepers at each end of the loop to mark the fouling points; this is a small proto-typical feature that is rarely modelled, yet very simple to do.
Barry Poultney

track and just played around with them on the piece of Sundeala until I arrived at the track plan shown. Having found that it fitted, I framed the Sundeala with 3 by 1 inch wood. I decided that I could trans-port the main board in one piece in the Maestro I then owned, which made the electrical side easier and also the setting up at shows.

The fiddle yards were also made from Sundeala framed with 3 by 1 inch wood. The main board rested on two trestles, and the two fiddle yards were joined to it by coach-bolts and rested on their own legs at each end, also fixed by coach-bolts. At exhibitions there was a shelf made of three-quarter-inch chipboard, which rested on the trestles at the rear of the layout. As can be seen from the track plan, it was possible to exhibit the layout in three different forms, although that never happened!

The track on the main board was all 0-16.5 Peco. In the fiddle yard it was a mixture of 0-16.5 track and OO gauge points, with adjustments being made for the thickness of the sleepers by using cork sheet where necessary. The track was pinned directly to the board and ballasted after the wiring had been completed.

The ballast was applied loose, then soaked with a 50/50 mixture of Resin W glue and water with one or two drops of washing-up liquid added to break down the surface tension. After being left to set for 24 hours, it was very firmly fixed.

The points were operated by welding rod of a diameter that fitted exactly into the hole in the Peco point tie-bar. The points in the fiddle yard were worked by hand.

Above right The real Brynglas ground frame, upon which the block post on the layout is based. This is a wooden shed with sliding windows to the front and one end. The walls are covered with roofing felt and cut and overlapped as shown. *Author*

Right Another small-layout prototype from the Talyllyn Railway, Quarry Siding Ground Frame. Outside the door is a drum to store water and, more importantly, the white sighting board; the blockman waves a green or yellow flag across the front of the board to make it easier for the loco crew to see it. *Author*

Scenery
The station building was scratchbuilt from Plasticard. It was not an exact replica of Brynglas station, being based more on Rhydyronen, the previous station on the line.

The goods shed was the side of an Ossett Mouldings engine shed kit with a roof made of Plasticard sheet to which corrugated Plasticard sheeting was glued.

The block post (signal box to the uninitiated) was scratchbuilt from Plasticard and loosely based on that

at the real Brynglas. The low-relief buildings hiding the switch gear were made of hardboard covered with Plasticard sheets of various kinds, and the water tower was an Airfix kit mounted on a base made from balsa wood and Faller embossed stone paper. The back scene was from Peco.

Examples of detail are the birds on the station and goods shed roofs, the allotment by the water tower, the coal lorry with a flat tyre and the spare being fitted watched by the man on the bike, and the white painted sleepers at each end of the loop, marking the fouling points.

The scene at the block post is also of interest as there is a tent (apparently belonging to the Talyllyn Railway volunteer - most irregular), and the Talyllyn Training Officer is watching to see if the trainee blockman is properly holding the yellow flag in front of the siting board, for a train coming into the loop. The blockman is leaning against the block post with his hands in his pockets, being surplus for the time being.

Electrical control

As usual, I wanted to keep this as simple as possible, and the feeds and dead sections are shown in the plan. Connections between the main board and the two fiddle yards were by heavy-duty multi-pin plugs and sockets, which I acquired at an Oxford MRC auction many years ago (I knew they would come in useful one day!). For ease of access all the electrical switches were set into the backscene on the main board and were hidden by low-relief buildings. The AC and DC inputs were beneath the layout and the hand-held controller was connected to the main board by a five-pin DIN plug and socket.

I made a mimic layout using very narrow chart tape on a piece of white laminate glued to the backscene, and the numbers of the switches were all marked for ease of operation.

As the layout was relatively small, I incorporated a number of working scenic features, one of which was an electrically operated gate, using a small electric motor mounted vertically beneath the board with the gate-post directly attached to the spindle; it was operated through the controller. There were also electrically operated uncouplers (Repa from Howes of Oxford) and two colour light signals.

Operation

At exhibitions the layout was operated to a sequence timetable, once again written out on cards that were flipped over on the cut-down back of an old ring-binder.

Brookhurst

This was a simple point-to-point layout that I built in 1978 with my elder son Justin when he was 8 years old. The idea of the layout was to involve him as much as possible, and he did as much as a boy of his age could be expected to do towards its construction.

It was again built with a view to exhibitions, and was also intended to show what can be achieved by the average modeller or newcomer to the hobby who builds a layout with his young son or daughter. Therefore I used easily obtainable material in the hope that newcomers could be encouraged to progress towards the heights of our hobby.

Baseboards and trackwork

The layout measured 9 ft by 1 ft 4 in and folded in half for storage and transport. The baseboards, being very important, were made by a carpenter friend of mine and a simple sketch of how the board folded is shown in the diagram opposite.

The track was all Peco Streamline, which I laid and wired with help from Justin. When the wiring was checked and found satisfactory, Justin ballasted the whole layout (except the points, which I did to avoid the glue sticking to the working parts) with loose ballast stuck on to white PVA glue applied previously between the sleepers. This was a somewhat tedious job, but it was worth it in the end, particularly on a small layout.

Then followed the point rodding. This was made from bicycle spokes, which ran under the baseboard. Each spoke was bent at right angles at both ends, to fit into the hole in the tie-bar at one end and form a handle at the other over which was fitted a piece of dowelling for easy holding. Being Peco points, they worked by a simple push-pull action.

Scenery

The backscene on the station baseboard was hardboard with a brick arch paper stuck to it. That which hid the fiddle yard was again hardboard with sky paper and trees cut from Hamblings and Peco backscenes on the top part, while the bottom part depicted a dairy ('Justin Paul Bros' - the names of my two sons, and a virtual crib from Peter Denny's Crispin Paul Bros!). The dairy and the buildings at the back of the goods platform were low-relief buildings made from the sides and ends of Airfix engine sheds.

The station platform was made from hardboard covered with Plasticard paving stone sheet suitably cut, and the station building was a Superquick example that Justin was given. He painted the platform

Plan of Brookhurst, and a diagram showing how the layout folded.

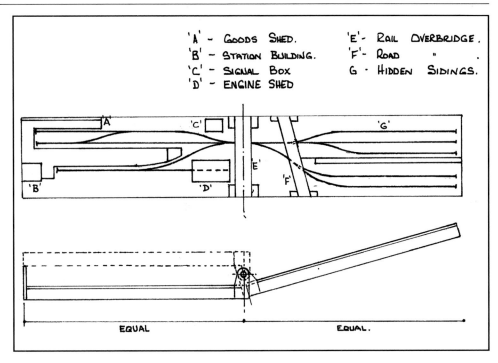

'A' – GOODS SHED.   'E'– RAIL OVERBRIDGE.
'B' – STATION BUILDING.   'F'– ROAD   "
'C' – SIGNAL BOX   G · HIDDEN SIDINGS.
'D' – ENGINE SHED

EQUAL   EQUAL.

surface with a mixture of paint and turps, which looked quite effective, and we then added various people, luggage, seats and gas lamps, etc, to give it some life. The signal box was also given to Justin, and was made by Merit.

The road to the coal staithes, engine shed and allotments was made from Polyfilla, which, before it was dry, had Matchbox toys pushed up and down it to simulate wheel tracks in the poor surface that we were intending to portray. Justin painted this black and also made the Airfix engine shed, which we both had a hand in painting. The rocky undulating ground on the other baseboard was made from broken pieces of Sundeala board, which was then covered with medical lint. This was already dyed green and brushed with diluted PVA, then scenic covering was sprinkled on and lichen bushes added in various places to break up the expanse of pure green.

The folding hinges were covered by two piers made of hardboard and covered with brick paper on which was mounted an Airfix girder bridge that Justin made. The other bridge, which covered the entrance to the hidden sidings, was made from two Peco girder bridges stuck to a piece of hardboard, and rested on the rocky hills at the front of the layout and a stone pier at the rear, which served to hide the switch panel for the hidden sidings (see the photograph on page 39).

I think the part of the scenery that gave Justin most pleasure was the allotments located between the track and the undulating ground on the hidden sidings board. He marked these out himself, sprinkled on the scenic covering, made the fence from fishing line and Slaters fence-posts, and located the men working. Although it was, and still is, quite unusual to find allotments by the trackside, I think, with hindsight, it is a pity that we hid part of it from the viewing public at exhibitions.

That describes how the layout was initially built, but no model is ever really finished and it was not long before we started to change and improve things.

It was in the improved condition that the layout was exhibited at the 1979 National Model Railway Exhibition at Central Hall, Westminster.

All Saints depot

I built this layout in the early 1980s in a modelling room measuring 8 ft 6 in by 7 ft 3 in. By moving the traverser it allowed continuous and end-to-end running .

Baseboards and trackwork
The baseboards were once again made for me by a friend and incorporated a useful workbench. The boards were of conventional design, using 2 by 1 inch timber surfaced with Sundeala boards. The workbench was screwed underneath and was made from half-inch chipboard.

The main-line track was ballasted in my now usual way using proprietary ballast and a 50/50 mixture of Resin W glue and water. However, in the MPD and other yard areas I used a mixture of Polyfilla and powder paint, as described for a previous layout.

Scenery
The embankment was made from polystyrene packing covered with a layer of Mid-Roc which, when dry, was covered with a grass mat. The embankment was topped with a fence made, as before, from Slaters fencing-posts and fishing line. The station side of the layout (all 8 ft 6 in of it!) was bounded by a length of Brittains walling, while on the MPD side the

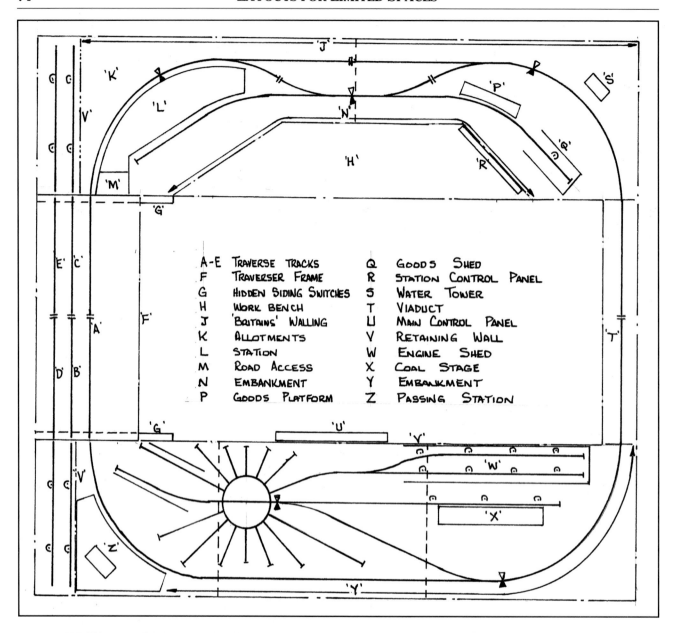

A–E TRAVERSE TRACKS   Q GOODS SHED
F   TRAVERSER FRAME   R STATION CONTROL PANEL
G   HIDDEN SIDING SWITCHES S WATER TOWER
H   WORK BENCH   T VIADUCT
J   'BRITAINS' WALLING   U MAIN CONTROL PANEL
K   ALLOTMENTS   V RETAINING WALL
L   STATION   W ENGINE SHED
M   ROAD ACCESS   X COAL STAGE
N   EMBANKMENT   Y EMBANKMENT
P   GOODS PLATFORM   Z PASSING STATION

Above All Saints depot.

Left All Saints depot was built in an extension to my garage. The workbench can be seen immediately in front of the station on the far side; this was a good arrangement and one that I would consider again if I was building a layout with operating space in the middle. *Joe Prestidge*

backscene was made of plywood covered with Slaters brickpaper to simulate a retaining wall. The concealed sidings were hidden by a hardboard backscene to which was stuck an Ossett Mouldings rock-face, suitably painted with sky above it.

The buildings were relatively straightforward. The station was a Prototype Models kit of an LMS station, and the goods unloading area was simply a Plasticard roof covered with slate paper and supported by a balsa wood frame. The water tower was an OO Airfix kit supported on a stone pier made from a balsa wood frame covered in Faller stone card.

The engine shed was a lean-to affair, the wall being made in a similar way to the water tower support, ie balsa wood and Faller card. The roof was made of Plasticard covered mainly with slate paper cut into strips and overlapped, but the front part was covered with Slaters corrugated tin sheeting to make it look as though it had been repaired.

The station building at the passing station was an Airfix timekeeper's hut with the front cut out; it gave a very presentable impression of a passenger shelter, particularly as I had fitted a seat all round the inside wall and placed a number of seated figures on it.

There was another building similar to the goods shed in the MPD, in addition to the engine shed. Also in this area I mounted two more Airfix water tower kits on the framing from the Airfix signal gantry and supported them on legs. The yard was then covered with the usual sort of litter, ash, coal, wheels, loco parts, etc, and water cranes and a coaling stage were added. In the corner of the station board I made some allotments; this was a useful way of filling the corner, and they looked quite effective.

Electrical control

The wiring was carried out once the boards had been erected and the track laid. There were three controllers:

- the main controller, which could control the whole layout, except for the traverser.
- the station controller, which could control the station side of the layout, independently of the main controller, and
- the traverser controller.

A DPDT switch was fitted to the main panel; in one position it meant that the main controller covered everything, in the other that the main controller covered the MPD half of the layout and the station controller the station half of the layout. The split between the two halves was on the viaduct.

The traverser controller was preset to level and direction depending on which controller was sending

the loco on to the traverser. The station controller had its own small panel with switches to cover its area.

Operation

The layout had a great deal of operating potential. Each of the rear two roads on the traverser was split into two, so the traverser could hold four trains, plus another if the front track was not being used as a through road. There was further storage (four roads) in the area behind the rock-face, and these could hold up to eight trains depending on length (more usually five or six).

A timetable was worked out for the layout, but before it had been operated a great deal the 'alterations bug' bit me and it was dismantled. It had lasted 4½ years and I had enjoyed building it, but somehow it didn't meet my requirements, probably because it couldn't be exhibited.

Old Milverton Sidings

This was a minimum space, minimum cost layout. The main portion had formed a small extension to a previous permanent layout and, for some reason or other, I was loth to break up this small board, so I decided to make a fiddle yard of the same size, bolting it to the original board to give a layout measuring 3 ft 6 in by 1 ft.

I really enjoyed building this layout; I have always found great enjoyment from building a small layout and adding scenic detail. I cannot believe those who say that they do not have space for 7 mm scale modelling - if they can't find a space 3 ft 6 in by 1 ft, they're not trying!

Baseboards and trackwork

The photograph overleaf shows the complete layout, and the joint between the two boards can be seen under the rear wheels of the milk float. Obviously, with a layout of such a small size it was unnecessary to split it for transport, and the two boards were permanently joined together.

The boards were made in the usual manner with 2 by 1 inch timber and Sundeala board surfaces. A hardboard facia was pinned to the ends and front of the two boards after they were bolted together; this was subsequently painted matt brown.

The track was standard Peco OO. In the sidings the point and track were buried in 'gunge' made from Polyfilla and powder paint, thus covering all the sleepers. In the fiddle yard this was clearly unnecessary. The points were operated manually using welding rod of a diameter that fitted into the hole in the tie-bar.

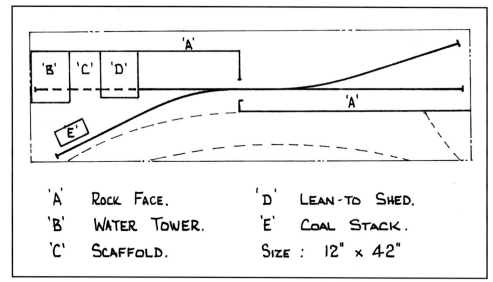

'A'   ROCK FACE.   'D'   LEAN-TO SHED.

'B'   WATER TOWER.   'E'   COAL STACK.

'C'   SCAFFOLD.   SIZE : 12" x 42"

Above A view of the whole of Old Milverton Sidings, showing the detail in front of the fiddle yard. The milk float is strategically positioned to hide the join between the two boards. *Joe Prestidge*

Left A plan of the layout.

Scenery

The backscene of the layout was of hardboard, and to this was stuck Ossett Mouldings rock-face painted grey, which I had used before. Above the backscene was an additional piece of thin plasticard on to which I stencilled the name of the layout; to avoid the lettering being smudged, I then sprayed it with hair lacquer, which proved effective.

As always, on a layout of this size it is very important to pay a lot of attention to scenic detail, both from the point of view of the builder and the exhibition viewer. The two main structures on the siding were a water tank and a lean-to shed; the former was an OO Airfix kit supported on a framework of Airfix signal gantry pieces and timber, while the lean-to was made of a wooden framework and Plasticard with roof laths of Slaters Microstrip. There was also a coaling stage and a small coach body used as a mess hut. Between the water tank and shed I built some scaffolding from welding rod and Plasticard.

The workmen on the scaffolding were bought for 1p each at a Toy Fair; in fact, I bought about 15 of them at the same time. Altogether there were nearly 40 figures on the layout, but it didn't look overcrowded.

The yard itself had typical clutter such as tools, lamps, oil cans, chimneys, wheels and oil drums. The coaling stage was made from half a Japanese military bridge kit to which was added coal and a corrugated tin roof. This may sound an odd mixture, but it looked quite reasonable. The yard was bounded by the usual fence of Slaters fenceposts and fishing line, and there was a gate into the yard just where the line disappeared into the fiddle yard.

The road was the scenic effect with which I tried to join together the two halves of the layout, and it also had a fence dividing it from a strip of grass on the front edge of the board.

To add to the viewers' interest I always displayed a list of the major scenic detail items, effectively challenging the viewers to find them. It never failed! These included the small working colour light signal; the foreman in the white coat supervising the workmen on the scaffolding platform; the oil can and lamps by the water crane; the saw lying on top of the oil drum in the yard; the man leaning on the fence; the man leaning on the broom and the man using the pneumatic drill in the road-mending party; the man pasting the poster on the hoarding, complete with bucket; the 'Road Up' sign; the bicycle by the road works; and the two crates of milk on the milk float.

Electrical control

On a layout of this size and design it would be impossible to have any complicated electrics! In fact, there was one feed and a dead section on each of the tracks. The control panel was built into the back of the layout and the power input was through two single plugs and sockets. The main feed was through an on/off switch built into the fiddle yard board, so the layout could be 'turned off' without any unplugging. In addition there was a small two-aspect colour light signal, which had its own separate feed and switch.

Operation

The operating potential of Old Milverton Sidings was somewhat limited to say the least! It was the only exhibition layout I have ever built that did not have an operating sequence - it was too simple! However, that was not the object of building it - I like building locos and it served as an easily transportable means of displaying some of them rather than as static models. Nevertheless, it was very relaxing just to shunt locos round the yard and it had the added bonus of only requiring a relatively small number of locos and the odd wagon or two, thus keeping transport and insurance costs down, which is always a factor to be considered by Exhibition Managers.

The whole layout, stock box, 'exhibition box', lighting, etc, were easily transported in my Metro, together with my elder son Justin.

Milverton

I built this layout with my younger son Paul. I say *with*, but I must admit that Paul was only 6½ years old at the time, so he did not do too much, but he did as much as could be expected of him. It was almost identical to a plan shown in the October 1978 *Railway Modeller* except that I added an extra siding for an engine shed, which ran off the loop towards the road bridge.

Baseboards and trackwork

The baseboard was made from 2 by 1 inch timber and ⅜ inch Sundeala board. The track and pointwork were Peco.

Ballast was sprinkled on loose, then a 50/50

mixture of Resin W glue and water was dropped on to it from an eye-dropper. After it had set hard the excess ballast was removed with a vacuum cleaner.

The points were again operated using welding rod of a diameter that fitted into the holes in the tie-bars without any adjustment. The rods were a straight push-pull and were located opposite the points that they controlled.

Uncoupler ramps were made from the clear plastic supplied to glaze the Airfix platform canopy.

Scenery

Once the track was laid, the facia board was cut out and fixed to the baseboard. Next the road was laid in and the embankments formed using damp newspaper and Mod-Roc. Initially I painted this with green gloss paint and covered it with flock powders, but this was not very successful, so I brushed off the flock and used scenic mat, and this looked quite effective. The road surface was obtained by painting the plywood matt black and shaking on household scouring powder while the paint was still wet - it looked surprisingly realistic. The tunnel mouth was by Merit.

The buildings were all from kits; the station building, the engine shed, the platform and three small huts were all Airfix, while the coal staithes were made from balsa wood and card. The station fencing was by Ratio and there were various other accessories by Merit and Peco. The people were from Airfix and Subbuteo - I found that the latter's football spectators were quite useful for placing on station platform seats.

The advertisement hoarding seen in the photograph is of interest because it was made from two painted Airfix garage doors and some plastic sprue to form the three 'legs'.

The vehicles were all repainted Matchbox models.

Plan of Milverton.

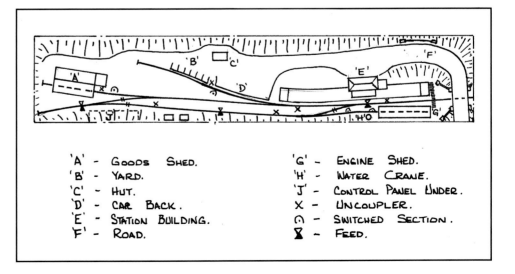

'A' - GOODS SHED.
'B' - YARD.
'C' - HUT.
'D' - CAR BACK.
'E' - STATION BUILDING.
'F' - ROAD.

'G' - ENGINE SHED.
'H' - WATER CRANE.
'J' - CONTROL PANEL UNDER.
X - UNCOUPLER.
∩ - SWITCHED SECTION.
Ⴟ - FEED.

A view of my son Paul's Milverton layout, an effective little model that gave us much pleasure. It was operated from the front, which seemed to be appreciated by exhibition viewers. Note the advertising hoardings on the embankment - a simple feature to model. Note also the mistake we made in folding the grass mat and the Mod-Roc over the top of the hardboard fascia board - this looked untidy and should have been trimmed off flush. *Joe Prestidge*

Electrical control

A small hinged control panel was fitted into a hole cut out under the embankment. The panel was laid out in a diagrammatic form using toggle switches for feeds and push-button switches for dead sections. Power to the panel was through a two-pin plug and socket, which connected to the controller.

The Wharf

This was a small 7 mm narrow gauge layout measuring 6 ft by 1 ft 4 in. It was originally made on two boards, each 3 feet long, but very quickly I decided that it was easy to carry in my Metro in one piece with the front passenger seat folded down. Therefore the two boards were permanently bolted together and a strip of 1 inch square wood screwed along the 6 foot lengths for stability; this saved any problems with cross-baseboard joints.

Baseboards and trackwork

The boards were made of 2 by 1 inch timber topped by ⅜ inch heavy density fibreboard, which is not unlike chipboard in its hardness but is much smoother.

The track was all Peco 0-16.5 with the exception of one point in the hidden sidings, which was a Peco OO gauge example. The track in front of the hidden sidings was set in Polyfilla to match the height of the ground level of the wharf; the remainder was ballasted normally. Between the tracks in some areas there was a mixture of 'gunge', ie Polyfilla mixed with black powder paint and trowelled directly on to the baseboard surface.

The points were operated by push-pull welding rods; each rod had a handle of dowel glued to the end.

Scenery

The front edge of the baseboard was disguised as a wharf-side and was covered with Faller card stonework suitably 'dirtied'. The usual wooden stanchions one sees on harbour walls were made of strips of square hardwood. At the end of the board were some steps going down to 'water' level; these were made from a Prototype Models signal box kit. The wharf surface was sheets of Slaters Plasticard setts painted grey and dirtied.

To receive short trains there was a small platform, and opposite this was a scrap dump, behind which were low-relief buildings made from hardboard covered in Slaters Plasticard brick or stone. Alongside them

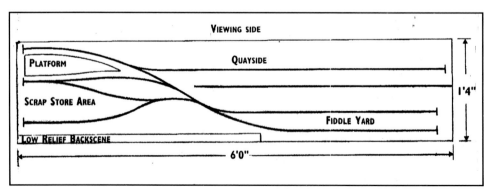

Plan of The Wharf. *Courtesy* British Railway Modelling

The railcar waiting at the very basic passenger platform at The Wharf. It is a modified San Francisco tramcar kit on a Lima chassis; the tarpaulin sheet at the front - in case of inclement weather - hides the motor. *Tony Wright*

Two vans waiting to be loaded on the wharf siding. Note the tarpaulins, the boats and the man about to climb the ladder - all little details that add to the picture. *Tony Wright*

Talyllyn (minus its cab) stands quietly on the siding by the scrap dump. The stacked metal advertising signs can be seen to the left of the loco. *Tony Wright*

and along the end of the layout there was a fence made from Faller card stuck to plywood, which was screwed to the baseboard frame.

There were two sheds on the wharf itself - one from Ossett Mouldings that I had bought a long time ago, and the other scratchbuilt from Plasticard. The hidden sidings were concealed by a backscene made from a cheap O gauge kit of the Talyllyn Railway's Wharf station. I laid the major part of the building out flat and mounted it on a piece of the same wood used for the baseboard surface. The wood was then cut to the shape of the building, which was coloured using felt-tip pens. Two of the removable buildings were made from the leftovers of the kit. Hence the name of the layout - The Wharf.

At the opposite end of the fence, at the platform end of the layout, there was a low-relief building and wall, and behind these I cut up Talyllyn Railway postcards to make a convincing backscene.

Here I must emphasise once again that on a small layout you have to have a lot of detail to keep people's attention. It is also enjoyable to model (at least for me!). A small Alphagraphix shed was used as the office of the scrap area behind the platform, and this included a workbench with the usual tools on it; against the low-relief buildings there were some enamelled signs stacked against one another, an idea I borrowed a *Model Railroader* magazine.

There were also other small items of detail such as chains on the wharf, two small boats, a man carrying a ladder, a man just about to climb a step-ladder, a ladder against one of the buildings, folded tarpaulins, and an oil drum on a support. All these added to the general picture.

Electric control
These were very straightforward and the control panel was simply a piece of hardboard screwed directly on to the rear of the board framework, hidden by removable buildings. The controller was a hand-held AMR plugged into a five-pin DIN socket. The AC was fed into two sockets, also incorporated into the panel.

Operation
At exhibitions and at home the layout was operated to a sequence timetable. The stock was carried in two stock boxes, and the layout was very quick and easy to set up - two trestles, two plugs, put on the frontal, put up the light and get out the stock. When we took The Wharf to exhibitions we were always ready to run very quickly, and on our way home at the end of the show within 20 minutes, having packed it all into the car again. To borrow a remark made by Edward Heath when he was Prime Minister - that is 'the acceptable face' of model railway exhibitions!

The Shed (Mark II)

This was my first standard gauge O gauge layout and depends heavily on the Heljan engine shed kit, hence its name. It can be worked as a Preservation Society engine shed, with locos coming on and off shed and the occasional wagons coming to and from the low-relief works that hides the fiddle yard. An alternative scenario is that the engine shed has been taken over as a wagon repair works, with wagons being brought in and out.

Baseboards and trackwork
There are two baseboards, each measuring 5 ft 6 in by 1 ft 9 in. It was originally intended that these should be transported to exhibitions bolted face to face through two end-pieces but, having used half-inch chipboard and 3 by 1 inch timber for the main framework, it is far too heavy and we use two cars instead of one. The cross-bracing is 3 by 1 inch timber, as I originally thought I might fit folding legs; however, I decided against that - even more weight!

The backscene is hardboard strengthened by 1 inch square timber. The fiddle yard pivots on a bolt and is lined up to the main track on to the layout by a domestic door bolt, which also gives electrical continuity. There are only two tracks in the fiddle yard, but

The Shed (Mark II). *Courtesy* British Railway Modelling

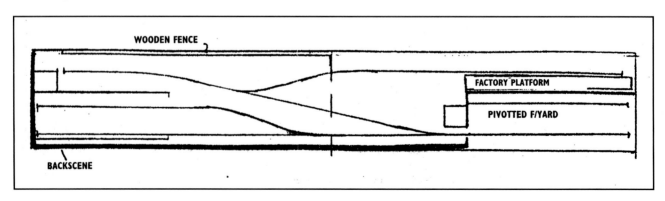

Locos on shed, including the front end of a 'Hymek'. *Tony Wright*

A tram loco waits to leave the factory siding with a short train. *Tony Wright*

The unnumbered 'Hymek' leaves the shed while the tram loco waits with its short train to leave the siding. A road-roller waits in the road. *Tony Wright*

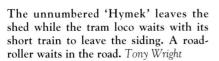

there is a shelf above it on which the spare locos or wagons can be stored.

Peco track and points are used, the latter being operated by welding rod with a glued-on dowelling handle to make push-pull operation easier.

The ballast was brushed on loose then held in place by soaking it with a 50/50 mix of Resin W glue and water with a few drops of washing-up liquid added to reduce surface tension. I do this using an eye dropper and it's surprising how quickly it can be done.

Scenery

The backscene was painted sky blue using emulsion paint - two sample 'matchpots' were more than enough for the whole job. On the board incorporating the hidden sidings, I used two factory backscenes with the sky paper cut off; these were stuck directly on to the painted backscenes in such a way that I obtained one long factory. Beneath that there are Langley retaining walls painted grey and suitably weathered.

In front of the hidden sidings there is a low-relief works made from the fronts of two Heljan engine shed kits and some of the side walls. A loading platform runs the length of the works siding, and at the end of the siding is a Faller card wall.

On the other board is the main Heljan engine shed kit and, behind it, another backscene also cut out and stuck directly on to the painted hardboard.

Leading up to the shed is a low-relief building, again made from the engine shed sides and roof parts. Between the tracks to the shed and inside the tracks there is the usual 'gunge' made from Polyfilla mixed with black powder paint.

In front of the tracks on the engine shed board there are various wagon bodies and, in front of them, a work area containing a lot of detail, including a workbench, a man sawing wood, and a welding set. Such features as this help the scenic effect because viewers have to look through the van bodies to see the tracks and the rolling-stock movements, which is what we often have to do in real life.

All along the front of this board is a fence made from strip wood glued to square timber verticals and horizontals. These 'planks' are glued on individually, so that some are broken, some have slipped and one area is in process of being renewed. On the other baseboard a post-and-wire fence has been being erected in front of the siding, but work has temporarily ceased as one of the workmen is underneath the dumper truck repairing it! Also on this board, to disguise the fiddle yard entrance, there is a small building, again from the engine shed kit, and mounted on the roof is an Airfix water tank. This not only serves its purpose but looks very effective.

Examples of detail on the layout include bicycles, speed restriction signs, Ratio telegraph poles, notice boards on buildings, ladders, small sheds, a relay box and a number of people in various poses.

Electrical control

The control panels (one on each board) are made from white-faced hardboard screwed to the backscene framing. Mimic track layouts are set out on them using ⅛ inch wide self-adhesive red tape, which gives an effective finish, with miniature switches set in the appropriate places.

The control panels are screwed to the top horizontal backscene frame; all the wires run under the baseboard and come through holes vertically above one another in the side of the main baseboard frame. The wires then run up to the panel inside rectangular plastic electric conduit, the front of which slides on or off; this ensures no loose wires and is extremely tidy. The cross-baseboard connections are by heavy duty multipin plugs and sockets.

The control panel on 'The Shed', showing the use of the plastic section conduit to bring wires from underneath the baseboard through the side frames up to the panel. It is a simple job to slide the front of the conduit down to gain access to the wires. *Martin Hewitt*

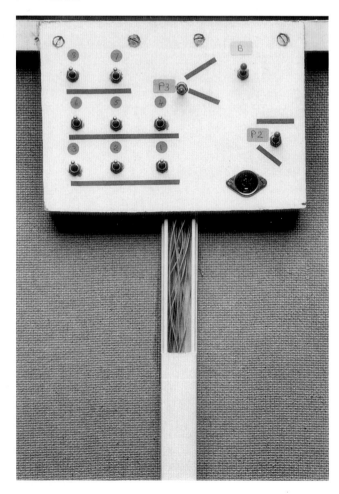

Initially I trusted the point blades to make the electrical contact when they were switched over, but this was a mistake and I had to add extra miniature switches to the panels to ensure proper contact.

There is one (three-aspect) signal on the layout, and this is operated by a rotary switch and powered by a separate small Mainline controller, which is no longer available.

The layout is controlled by a hand-held AMR controller, which plugs into a five-pin DIN socket. The main AC feed is into two sockets set in a piece of hardboard screwed to the cross-bracing of one of the boards.

The initial method of energising the fiddle yard tracks was by a 'wander lead' with a plug on the end, which was inserted into one of two sockets mounted on the side of the fiddle yard. However, this has been superseded by the use of a microswitch, which is much better and very reliable. This was a benefit of belonging to a club, as it was suggested by Peter Honeybone (a COVGOG member), who also provided the microswitch!

Small motive power depot

As we have seen, my narrow gauge loco shed (see page 65) was in a sense a 'pointless' layout - and here's another one! Like its predecessor its main feature is a traverser.

When I built 'The Shed' I had some spare parts of the Heljan engine shed kit left over, so I decided to see how small a layout I could build in O gauge using the same basic design and the left-over Heljan parts.

The shed on this new layout is really the fiddle yard, and the length of the layout was decided having taken into account three factors:

- the main tracks should be 36 inches long, thus avoiding cutting lengths
- the traverser should be 7½ inches long, which is quite sufficient for short-wheelbase locos
- it should easily fit into the back of a Metro, as both my elder son and I have these.

This meant that the baseboard size worked out at 45 by 22 inches. Who hasn't got space for an O gauge layout?

Baseboard and trackwork

The framework is 2 by 1 inch softwood, screwed together, and the surface is half-inch chipboard. The backscene is an integral part of the baseboard and is made from hardboard framed with half-inch square timber. Also attached to the backscene are shelves, also made from hardboard, for loco storage and other bits and pieces. The control panel is built into the back of the baseboard so the layout is completely self-contained. The baseboard is supported on an ingenious framework designed and made for me by one of my parishioners (see page 34).

The layout is held in place by two 'contijoiners', each having two holes drilled at right angles to the normal on one half so that the joiner can be used to join two faces in an 180-degree plane, rather than at right angles. The legs fold up and the framework is carried separately on its side behind the front seats of the car.

The traverser is simple but effective and works in exactly the same way as the one described earlier.

A close-up view of the traverser on my small MPD layout. It is 7½ inches long and runs on the threaded rod principle described on page 66. Underneath can be seen the inverted U-shaped bracket; nuts are welded on each leg, and they run along the rod. The current for the track is picked up by a copper-clad strip that rubs on the rails that can be seen supporting the traverser on both sides. *Martin Hewitt*

The loco on the left is a straight repaint of a Lima 0-4-0 by Mike Hewitt. The other is purely a 'fun loco' for the children at exhibitions, and is a Highfield kit mounted on a Lima 0-4-0 chassis. *Martin Hewitt*

The track is all set in a mixture of my usual 'gunge' consisting of Polyfilla mixed with white and black powder paints to achieve a grey colour. This is spread all over the track and the baseboard surface with an old knife and my forefinger and allowed to dry, after which the surplus can be removed.

Scenery

The rear backscene consists of Heljan engine shed kit parts in low relief together with other Heljan wall parts. The right-hand backscene is a section of Langley retaining wall, above which is a backscene adapted from an old one that I had in stock. The left-hand backscene again uses parts from the old one, and the wall is Prototype Models brick paper mounted on a wooden frame and very much weathered.

Along the front of the layout is a Ratio SR concrete fence, and my youngest son, Paul, has used his talents to apply some graffiti to it, which I think is very effective.

Electric control

This is very simple. There is one feed for each track, and each track is divided into five sections (ie one feed and four dead sections). Provision is made in the control panel for a hand-held controller to be plugged in. There are also two sockets for the wheel-cleaning brush and two for the AC feed. To complete the electrical picture, a solitary floodlight bulb is mounted on a single pole screwed to the back of the layout for exhibitions.

Operation

The MPD is a very easy layout to take to shows. As already stated, the supporting frame is stowed behind the front seats of the car, the rear seats are folded once and the layout goes in lengthways on the right-hand side. On the left-hand side go two plastic stacking boxes with the usual exhibition paraphernalia (controllers, frontal, light bulbs, transformers, tools, etc), three small stock boxes, a stool and a lighting pole. The second operator travels in the passenger seat. Setting up and dismantling is quick and easy.

As always I operate the MPD to a sequence timetable written out on cards mounted on the back of an old cut-down ring-binder.

Writing about the small layouts I have built over the years, I realise how my standards have improved and also how what is on offer from the trade has improved. In addition, like many others in our hobby, I have changed scale from OO to 009 to O-16.5 and O. As I said earlier, building small layouts makes it easier to keep modelling to the same standard on a layout. It also enables you, if you wish, to change scales with relative ease without having to destroy a large layout and all that goes with it! I admire people like Peter Denning and Ken Northwood who have built large masterpieces, but for whatever reason, it's just not for me. It's a good job we are all different!

Summer of '94
by Paul Towers

We now move on to layouts built by other modellers. Being deeply attracted to the Class 60 led to Paul Towers's interest in all heavyweight diesels and a determination to build a stabling point to enable him to depict them in model form.

A decision had to be made concerning which sector of Trainload Freight and which locos to have. About the only good thing to come out of the reorganisation of British Rail and Trainload Freight was that the locos on the yard could be mixed up!

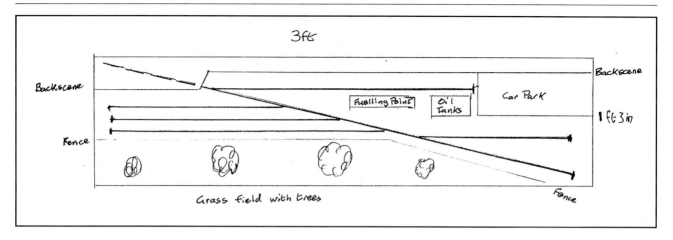

A rough sketch of 'Summer of '94'.

Beforehand it would have been remarkable to see a
Coal Sector loco on a steel train or two Class 37s
with differing sector markings hauling a tanker train,
but in the summer of 1994 this became common, so
the layout was born.

It was assumed that the stabling point had been
built on the yard of a former steel works. The
Bethlehem Iron & Steel Works existed but in the US,
and it is also assumed that there was one in this country, making this the Bethlehem Stabling Point. . .!

Baseboards and trackwork

The first job was to visualise the basic track plan and
operate it in the imagination. Paul rarely draws plans
on paper, adhering to the old adage that those who
draw meticulously detailed plans never lay a piece of
track! It was decided that the basic track plan should
fit into an area 3 ft 6 in or 3 feet long by 12 inches
wide, with another 3 inches for the controls behind
the backscene.

The first actual job was to cut and connect up the
track before even starting on the baseboard. Then it
would be known if the track plan would fit into 3 feet
or 3 ft 6 in; it was found that the former was OK, and
that there would be room for a fuelling point! The
design was such that if every space was used in the
stabling point some ten diesels could be accommodated!

The baseboard was constructed in a totally uncon-
ventional way, but one well tried and tested over
many years and layouts. The frame was made from
2 by 1 inch planed timber, with four side-pieces and
two cross-members, the latter with the 2-inch face
upwards. First these were joined with small plastic
shelf brackets to ensure that all pieces were at right
angles, then screwed together giving a strong square
baseboard.

Planks of half-inch-thick balsa were then laid on
top except for a section behind the scenes where the

An end-on view of the layout. *Paul Towers*

control panel would be located. The balsa was in turn
covered by ⅛-inch-thick self-adhesive cork floor tiles,
which help to deaden sound.

All track was Peco using small-radius 'electrofrog'
points, but it was decided to use mechanical operation rather than point solenoids. After much debate -
all of 5 minutes - the cork tiling was cut to provide a
slot running from the tie-bar to behind the scenes. A
thin length of spring steel wire was attached to the
tie-bar and brass tube threaded over it; the other end

coloured acrylic paint and flock glued on to it.

The surface where the track was going to be laid had previously been painted with dark grey acrylic paint, and this was used to colour the Polyfilla filling the point cable runs, looking in places as though somebody had dug up areas to lay drains or cables. The track was ballasted with 5:1 granite ballast and Cascomite and sprayed with water. The rails were painted and the ballast dirtied.

The field area was painted with brown acrylic paint then 'grass' was glued to it, and some sprinkled liberally around the depot. Trees were added to the field and cars to the upper car park, and both areas were given a liberal sprinkling of people studying the current railway scene!

The fuelling point and fuel tanks were added, together with railway

was bent to a right angle and a plastic tube fitted over it as a handle. The brass tube was then pinned down and the slot in the tiles filled with Polyfilla.

Scenery

The basis of the backscene is Foamex on to which is glued sky paper and, on top of that, a Townscene landscape depicting factories and countryside. The lower section is a retaining wall and a tunnel mouth. The retaining wall (stone) is actually for 4 mm scale, but it seemed a bit small for that and the N gauge was certainly too small. Cracks and spaces were filled with Polyfilla, then the whole thing painted with stone-

workers painted with high visibility clothing, some with an arm uplifted answering the driver's warning horn!

Electrical control

Wiring was conventional using single pole miniature switches and a common return feed. The two main feed switches and eight section switches were geographically located on the track plan.

Operation

Operation is at random depending on the operator's whim, but some form of pattern must emerge with the yard being fairly full at one stage and emptying slowly to fill again later.

All but three locos are Graham Farish, while the remaining three use Farish mechanisms.

Strangely, Sasquehanna and Clemens Landing
Three layouts by Richard Insley

The size of a layout usually determines scale, but scale rarely determines layout size. What, then, determines a layout's size? The size of the three layouts discussed here was determined by several factors, all loosely based on the question of storage or transportation. All three have subsequently grown or are growing, and again this growth is influenced by storage or transportation. In addition, each layout's problems led to improvements in the next layout.

Strangely (HoN 2.5)

Back in the early 1980s Richard Insley was modelling US N gauge on a fixed-to-the-wall 12 feet by 1 ft 5 in layout in the marital bedroom (note here a tolerant wife). His son, Charles, who was heavily into 009, suggested that they co-operate on a layout. Choice fell on a US narrow (2 feet) gauge layout. All other problems and tasks stemmed from that decision.

Essentially a 009 layout (but strictly speaking HoN 2.5), the decision was taken to build two 4 by 2 feet boards; one would be kept in the marital bedroom on a dressing table 3 by 2 feet - so here the size was determined by a piece of furniture! Bracing using 1½ by ½ inch timber was used, together with hardboard (big mistake). The second board was stored hanging on the wall, so 4 by 2 feet was a lucky choice.

Track is Peco 009 laid on to the hardboard then ballasted in the traditional manner (with diluted PVA adhesive). In time the hardboard has warped, giving the track unexpected undulations (just like the prototype, people are not told). Points, operated by the rod-in-tube method, are Peco N gauge with alternate

sleepers removed, although this was found to be unnecessary since hardly anybody realises that the points are N.

All the locomotives and stock are scratchbuilt on N gauge chassis - kits obtainable from the USA or Japan are too expensive. Buildings are either kits or scratchbuilt, all in plastic, and painted prior to assembly. To highlight or distress the brick, stone or wood, the building was painted then the paint wiped off in a roof-to-ground motion. Colours used were brown, grey, cream or brick red. The cream produces mortar lines on brick; the bricks are then coloured by using a normal rubber covered in brick red paint and dabbed on to the wall.

For scratchbuilt structures the basic materials were either Wills or Slaters Plasticard. The buildings were reinforced with cardboard or more recently 'featherboard' (light but strong) - the method is shown in the accompanying diagram. If the buildings were to have internal lighting, the walls were made lightproof either with 'featherboard' or black photographic paper. Weathering was achieved using chalks, dilute paint or Indian ink, fixed with matt or satin varnish spray.

A lot of research, photographic and video, was used to produce 'New England'-type houses, roads, trees, etc, for Strangely. The layout has as many HO people as possible; Preiser figures are used, with some repainted

Richard Insley's sketch showing the use of 'featherboard' to reinforce scratchbuilt buildings.

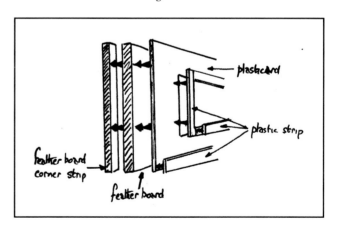

Plan of Strangely.

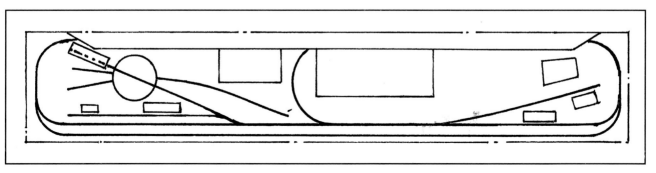

Views of the busy Main Street and the turntable and engine facilities at Strangely, showing the very effective scenic treatment. *All Martin Hewitt*

Merten figures. They are placed in positions that have a logical reason, and without their 'personal flagstones'. Since half the layout hangs on the wall, everything is securely glued down. All telephone poles are 'wired' with grey cotton, a process helped by careful consumption of 'Southern Comfort'!

Scenery is cork bark for rock faces, and grass mat laid then covered in different green scatter, while roads are black sandpaper weathered when in place. The first attempt at water was the traditional cast resin, which served for a year or so until some plastic sheet water from Faller was used. Trees are made by Richard's wife from either bottle brushes covered in glue then scatter material; wire twisted, covered in bath sealant, painted, then covered in glue and scatter; or dried hydrangea heads, covered in glue and scatter. All the trees are hairsprayed to hold the scatter in place, producing very fragrant trees. The first of the above methods produces only one type of tree, while the second method produces strong trees, but heavy for layouts that hang on walls; the third method produces cheap, light trees, but very delicate.

Only after Strangely was built was any consideration given to its transportation to exhibitions, a fact that has led over the years to some interesting operating problems and much bad language! To transport the layout a stacking frame has been constructed to fit the back of an Astra (Richard now always has to buy Astras, as anything bigger will not fit in the garage!). A diagram of the frame is shown below.

Strangely has since grown by a further 3 by 2 feet board that fits between the original boards. Since this addition was made in 1992 its construction has been influenced by subsequent layouts. It has hand-laid standard and narrow gauge crossovers and interchanges.

Sketch of the stacking frame used to carry Strangely in the back of the owner's car.

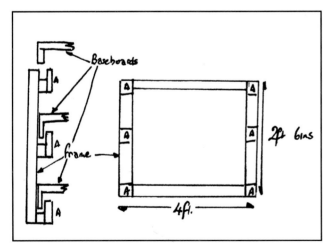

Sasquehanna (N)

This US N gauge layout, set in the late 1940s, began as two 5½ by 1½ feet boards. It was designed to fit across two bookcases and was not intended be an exhibition layout; since portability was therefore not an issue, both size and weight seemed unimportant. The boards were constructed of quarter-inch plywood and 1½ by ½ inch timber (nice and heavy, and non-warping). Later the layout was invited to exhibitions, and size and weight became a problem. First exhibitions had the 11-foot-long layout with 2-foot square fiddle yards at each end, but constantly walking from one end to the other quickly made this unacceptable. It then became 'L'-shaped with the addition of a 2-foot-square board in the middle; then finally a complete oval with a (slender!) operator in the middle. In its final incarnation it is 11 by 5 feet and requires tables. It is a 'swine' to transport and now has too many joints, since like Topsy it just 'growed'.

Techniques that were used on Strangely are used on this layout. There are three kit buildings but 24 scratchbuilt ones. The layout uses mirrors to give more depth to the 18-inch boards; these are not set parallel to the track and not where any trains can be seen passing. Any signs or other writing that will be seen in the mirror has to be written backwards (great fun!).

Vehicles posed a problem, as N scale US cars and vans of the 1940s are not easy to find. Then the film *Dick Tracy* came out and part of its marketing was small (very close to 2 mm) cheap 1940s motor cars. Repainted with minor changes they have been a godsend. Stock is modified Rivarossi, Bachmann, Minitrix, Kato and Con Cor, as well as some scratchbuilt on Grafar chassis.

Clemens Landing (N)

Of the three layouts, this is the most carefully planned for operation, storage and transportation.

Two boards are used, each 3 ft by 2 ft 6 in, curving to 2 feet so as to fit round the rear wheel arch of an Astra. This places the operator in a curve with all controls, point rods and switches easily to hand; and being only 1 ft 6 in from the front track, no standing up is required. In fact, this layout can cause 'bottom cramp'! The boards are transported by being bolted together, one above the other, as shown in the accompanying sketch. The only features not glued down are two large river boats.

Timber and plywood are used in the baseboards, with more bracing than previously used. The layout sits on a modified paste-table with (like Strangely) lighting fitted to the sides.

Research for the layout took over 12 months. Since it is set in Mississippi, USA, in 1858 (pre-Civil War

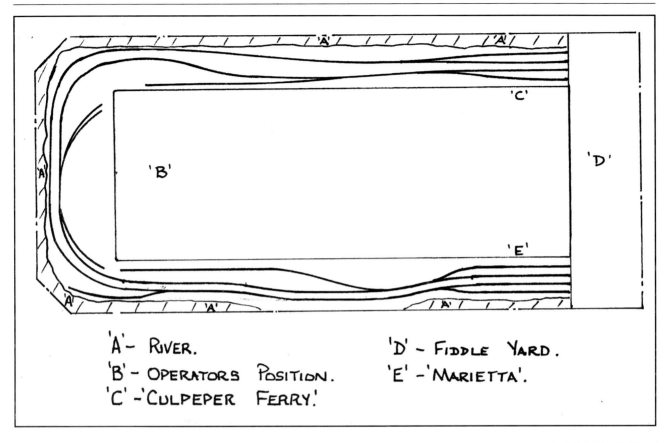

'A' – RIVER.   'D' – FIDDLE YARD.
'B' – OPERATORS POSITION.   'E' – 'MARIETTA'.
'C' – 'CULPEPER FERRY.'

Above Sasquehanna.

Right Carrying Clemens Landing's boards face to face.

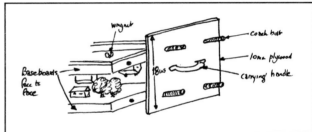

Below Clemens Landing, on the banks of the Mississippi.

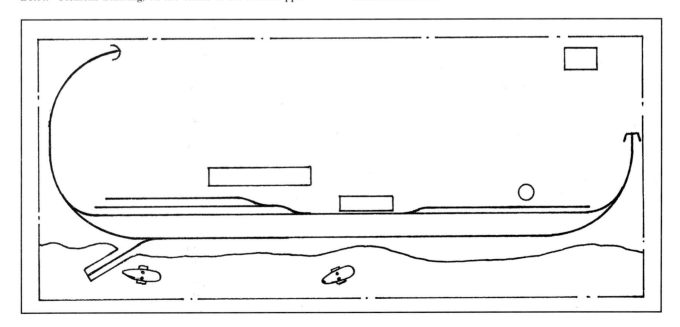

The river bank, houses and sheds at Clemens Landing. *Martin Hewitt*

slavery era) a lot of questions needed answering. Research had to be undertaken into such things as gauge (5 feet), slave quarters, houses, vehicles, normal dress of the time and paddle steamers. All had to be checked, using written documents, old photographs and videos of films like *Gone With The Wind* and *Roots*.

Stock is either heavily modified Bachmann 'Old Timers' in N gauge or scratchbuilt. Much research was also required as to the colour of 1858 US engines, whether they were outside or inside framed or outside or inside cylindered. The different positions of steam domes were limitless! All are wood burners and scale lumber proved a problem for some time until the right size birch twigs were obtained.

Since the layout features the Mississippi River at the front, all the non-river parts had to be raised, and since it had to be as light as possible, expanded polystyrene was used as a scenery base. Gone are the chicken wire, plaster, papier-mâché and toilet rolls of previous layouts, but as before grass mat paper and various green scatters are used as ground cover. Once again Richard's long-suffering wife produced a large

number of trees by the methods previously described. Roads are made of fine earth ballast spread directly on to undiluted PVA glue.

Road vehicles are all horse-drawn and most are suitably modified Langley models. As with previous layouts there are many people, all Preiser figures, which have to be painted; since 65 per cent of the figures are black there was no point in buying painted figures (and bankruptcy would have resulted!).

The river boats are either modified kits, depths raised by 5 mm, or scratchbuilt; the Kentucky keel boat took longer to research than to build. Since there are no kits of 'Deep South' buildings of the pre-Civil War period, all the buildings, ranging from a mansion to a barn, are scratchbuilt, using methods previously described. This time different lighting effects are obtained by glazing the windows in different coloured sweet papers. ('Yes, dear, I'm only eating these sweets for the windows!')

Again the layout is at time of writing expanding by 2 feet to add a reversing loop, several buildings and a saw mill - obviously owned by a T. Sawyer.

As each new layout has been constructed the question of storage, transportation and ease of operation has played a large part in the shape of the finished layout. These factors now greatly influence size, shape,

Two views of T. Sawyer's
sawmill at Clemens Landing.
Martin Hewitt

materials used, height of buildings, etc. Lightweight materials are essential if the layout is to be easily transported and buildings, etc, are not to fall off - nothing would be worse than having to rebuild the layout at the beginning of every exhibition. Gauge has not yet been affected, but S, O and G seem unlikely.

In building all three layouts, even as materials and methods have changed, the following simple rules have been applied:

- scenery as realistic as possible for the location
- enough dioramas to occupy the public when the trains do not run
- humorous names for the buildings and firms
- figures in realistic poses and positions (they need *not* be named)
- simple electrics - less to go wrong
- building and exhibiting must be *fun*!

The paddle-steamer *Mississippi,* and a close-up of the main street with a house,
shop and hotel, Clemens Landing. *Both Martin Hewitt*

Carron Road (EM)
by Nigel Bowyer

Nigel has always had a fascination for small layouts (he once abandoned a layout because it was too big!) and at exhibitions he is inevitably drawn to the small, intimate examples. He believes that the small layout is probably more difficult to build than a larger one - train lengths, clearances, loops, storage sidings and siding lengths are vital and have to be just right. Stock must be right as well, not too much of it otherwise the layout gets clogged. A train of short-wheelbase stock looks far better than a train of long-wheelbase wagons, so arrange the rolling-stock in small interesting groups, vary the height using vans and wagons, and vary the loads as well.

Nigel set his design criteria as follows:

- Maximum baseboard size not to exceed 48 by 20 inches to facilitate getting in and out of the loft
- Baseboards must be able to fit into a small family car for transportation
- Good presentation with its own independent lighting unit
- No 'dead' storage siding space
- Good shunting potential
- Urban rather than rural setting

Nigel has always been interested in the 'blue diesel' era; his previous layout, Dunbeath, was set on the Highland Lines during the 1970s. Scotland has always been his favourite region - even his best-loved Shakespeare play is *Macbeth*! He therefore made the decision to keep faith with Scotland, but to move from the Highland Lines to the former Caledonian territory in the Central Region of Scotland.

Carron Road.

Baseboards and trackwork

The baseboards were constructed using 2 by 1 inch softwood framing with a 9 mm ply top. The board with the sector plate was open-plan in construction so that it would be easy to pivot. The layout is supported by three folding trestles, which give a viewing height of 45 inches.

Cork tiles were used to cover the boards before any track was laid. Trackwork is C&L, and the points are operated with SEEP motors with a microswitch to change the polarity. The trackwork was wired and tested before ballasting. The ballast was laid dry, considerable care being taken to get it at the correct level. It was then sprayed with water, and a mixture of PVA glue and washing-up liquid dribbled on. When dry, it was painted with Humbrol track colour, and the oily patches where the locos stand were painted a gloss black. When all this was completed the track was tested again. Nigel is always amazed that his electrics actually work!

Scenery

Nigel now embarked on the part of the railway modelling that he enjoys the most, and from which he derives the most pleasure, the scenery and structures. Building an environment and creating an atmosphere is a mixture of proportion, composition, colour, texture and form. The positioning of the structures is all part of this process; there are many parallels with the creation of a painting. Indeed, many feel that creating a model railway is akin to creating a work of art.

The green areas owe everything to the methods described by Barry Norman in his book *Landscape Modelling*. The grassy areas were built up on foundation strips of old Wills scenic sheet packaging woven together - recycling materials! This was covered in a mixture of Polyfilla and PVA glue to prevent cracking, and was then painted with a thin coat of Burnt

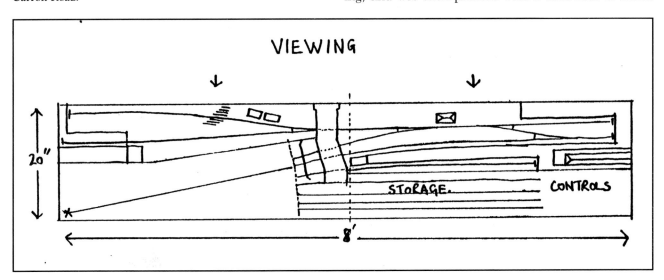

The relatively newly built warehouse is based on a building at Law Junction, and is constructed from Wills box cladding and corrugated sheets. The pallets, sacks and drums are from the Ratio range, and the wagon is a Parkside Dundas product. Slaters stone sheet forms the wall and platform facing. Note the ginger cat on the stack of pallets.

No 20201 enters Carron Road with a short trip working. The Lima model has buffer-beam details, screw-link couplings, Ultrascale wheels and has been weathered. The bridge was built from Wills bridge panels. The signal is by Eckon, and the signal box is based on that at Carfin, boasts a full interior, and was again built using Wills components. The line to the right leads to the small goods yard.

No 06005 shunts the small yard. It is a much modified Hornby model, with a new Constructeon chassis and A1 parts for the body, although the cab is still too wide. The 21T coal wagon is from the Parkside Dundas range. The small oil depot is in the foreground. *All Tony Wright, courtesy* Rail *magazine*

Umber. Small wads of carpet felt were soaked in a bucket of bleach, which leaves it a rather good dried grass colour, then tightly stuck down, again with PVA glue, and left to dry. The felt was then pulled off, leaving a slightly bald appearance, and painted with a mixture of Sap Green, Hookers Green and a touch of Burnt Sienna.

To break up the overall look, flocks and scenic textures from Set Scenes and Woodland Scenics were added using display mount aerosol as the adhesive. Small areas were sprayed through shapes torn out of newspaper and the foam flock sprinkled on to suggest the different colours and textures found on an embankment. Lichen formed the basic shape for the bushes, again sprayed with display mount adhesive then dipped in an old yoghurt carton of foam flock powder before being carefully positioned on the embankment. Heavier-textured foam flock was carefully glued between the sleepers in the goods yard to create the rather run-down, overgrown appearance of the layout.

All other buildings and structures were built using Plasticard and the excellent Wills scenic sheets; Nigel particularly likes the corrugated iron and asbestos sheets. Some of the buildings are imaginary, others were based on prototypes found in Central Scotland. The station building was based on that at Lesmahagow, and was built from plans in *Railway Modeller* of April 1970. The signal box was inspired by plans in the book *The Signal Box, A Pictorial History* and is based on the small boxes at Carfin and Benhar Junction. The prototype also boasts a zinc roof, modelled in Plasticard. It also has a fully modelled interior, but alas only the operators can see this.

The other structures take their inspiration from photographs rather than plans. The goods shed had its birth in a photograph of a building at Law Terminal from Silver Link's *Freight Only* series of books. The small oil terminal was constructed using Nigel's own holiday photographs of the facilities at Oban and Mallaig. Holidays are a good source of material, although Nigel hears frequent groans of 'not another station' from the rest of the family.

The retaining walls are sheets of Slaters random stone painted and weathered with black and white emulsion. The bridge in the centre of the layout, built using Wills bridge panels, provides a scenic break and was inspired by photographs in L. V. Woods's book *Bridges for Modellers*. Nigel spends a great deal of time painting and weathering until he gets the overall effect he requires, where the buildings and the landscape blend naturally with each other and there are no dominant features.

Rolling-stock, display and operation

The rolling-stock is a mixture of kit-built Parkside Dundas, Ratio, and modified proprietary Lima and Hornby items. All the stock is weathered to a variety of degrees, from dirty to very dirty! Nigel uses both paint and Carrs weathering powders. All stock is fitted with either instanter or screw-link couplings, which at the end of a long exhibition day can be trying, but they do look good.

The locomotives reflect both the era and location - Classes 06, 08, 20, 26 and 27, with occasional visits from Classes 37 and 47. The 06 is a much modified Hornby model, and the 08 a Modern Outline Kit, both built by Aidan Houlders to whom Nigel is indebted. The rest are Lima models fitted with Ultrascale wheels, buffer-beam details, fan grilles, snowploughs and wire handrails. They have been renumbered and weathered.

Nigel feels strongly about presentation and prepares thoroughly for each exhibition - building model railways requires dedication! It is impossible to calculate the hours that Nigel spent building Carron Road. Therefore it is of paramount importance that each time Carron Road is exhibited, it is presented as well as possible. It has its own lighting unit, which runs the length of the layout and displays the nameboard. Daylight bulbs (obtained from the local art shop) are used to give soft light. The black curtains that cover the front and sides, and hide all the paraphernalia connected with exhibiting, are always ironed before an exhibition and are carried as neatly as possible. The track and all the loco and wagons wheels are thoroughly cleaned before each outing, and any repairs are also carried out. If the public is paying to look at the layout its presentation and operation should always be of the highest order.

Building Carron Road gave Nigel a great deal of pleasure, as well as a little pain! The labour was all his, but others gave, and in some cases still continue to give, great support and encouragement. Nigel owes a considerable debt of gratitude to Chris Mansell, who offered great support and many suggestions during the building phase, as well as help at exhibitions. He is also grateful to Aidan Houlders who built the diesel shunters, and also helps at exhibitions. His thanks go to John Lunn for help at exhibitions, and finally to his family, for their patience and support for 'Karen Rhode'!

Ditchling Green
by Gordon Gravett

This layout was built several years ago to satisfy a number of interests and criteria, not all directly associated with model railways. Gordon's first 7 mm scale layout had been a narrow gauge project, built after a number of years 'out of the hobby'. A lot had changed during the 1970s and early '80s, so this new layout was very much a learning exercise, trying out different motors, controllers and scenic ideas, all of which had improved so much during this period. After a very pleasant few years developing and exhibiting 'Llandyref', thoughts were turning again to something new.

When discussing O gauge the first thing that comes to mind is the space it takes up - so much of it. How often do we hear the words 'I'd love to build in O gauge, but I haven't the space'? These words were always present when Ditchling Green was passing through its embryonic state, together with the question 'If an O gauge layout was designed to fit a smaller space and the limitations accepted, would it display sufficient interest for the paying public - and the operators?'

It was with this question in mind that doodles, sketches and eventually plans showed that something may be possible. The location was to be rural Sussex, near Lewes in the South Downs. Gordon lived in Sussex for his first 20 years so the layout was in part to be a nostalgia trip back to his early train-spotting days, when you could count the number of cars in the street on one hand - the mid-1950s.

Although best known for the multitudes of green electric units, the Southern Region retained a number of pre-Group (as well as more modern) steam classes for freight and branch use up to the early 1960s. Of these, ex-London, Brighton & South Coast locos were regularly seen around Three Bridges and Brighton. If modelled these would, hopefully, convey some of the local railway atmosphere to the layout.

Although limited for space it was decided from the outset that the scene was to go beyond the railway fence to show features that would help locate it. This would include the typical South East England architectural styles, tile-hung walls, half-hipped roofs and the use of flint as a building material.

The sketches and doodles soon showed that the track layout was going to have to be very simple or it would totally dominate such a small scene. The plans were pruned down to the bare essentials for a workable layout and the proportions arranged to give a reasonably uncluttered appearance.

To add interest for both the onlooker and the operator, a small nar-

Left Prototypes for the typical South East of England architectural styles used in the 'Ditchling Green' area - note the half-hipped roofs and tile-hung walls. *Gordon Gravett*

Below Ditchling Green.

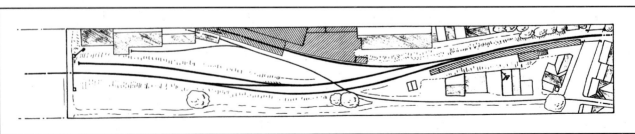

row gauge industrial line was included to run along one of the roads and to cross the 'main' line before disappearing into a ramshackle collection of sheds.

Trains were going to have to be very short on such a limiting layout - the run-round facility would only accommodate two coaches (at a pinch) or five short-wheelbase goods vehicles. This was, however, considered to be acceptable traffic for a rural branch line such as this. Every so often, when the line was quiet, a narrow gauge train might work its way through the scene.

Baseboards and trackwork

With the parameters set, the baseboards were built to enable safe transit and relatively easy assembly and dismantling. In an attempt to keep weight to a minimum, ply was used in the major part of the construction, although Gordon considers that the whole ensemble is still very heavy.

Three baseboards contain the scenic part of the layout and these, with a protective endplate

Class 'C2X' No 32527 standing on the narrow gauge crossing. These locos were seen all over Sussex and this model in made from brass. *Gordon Gravett*

attached, are arranged to stack as one unit for transportation, with the top board of the three inverted. This makes a completely enclosed unit with everything well protected. Gordon is of the opinion that virtually all the damage that is inflicted on model railway layouts occurs during moving and transporting: 'Having spent so much time and effort, enjoyable as it is, on producing a model, I think that taking care that it is well protected when it is finished is paramount.'

The storage yard was designed as a turntable to store four complete trains. With the same thought in mind that stock only usually gets damaged when being handled, even by very safe hands, the storage yard was designed for 'hands off' operation. With the train length very much restricted on the layout, the storage turntable is only 4 feet in diameter. Construction was kept to the very basic using white 'Contiboard' for both the deck and the base, and a very sophisticated quarter-inch nut and bolt as a pivot! The sliding surfaces were rubbed over with candle wax when being assembled (about five years ago) and have worked well ever since.

At the time of building Ditchling Green, Gordon decided to build a separate trestle unit to support this

Class 'A1X' No 32636 was built from a Vulcan kit. This loco was at Newhaven Docks before being bought and preserved on the Bluebell Railway. Note the superb effectiveness of the scenic vegetation. *Gordon Gravett*

Ground surfaces were finished with textured earth or tarmac coloured paint as appropriate. The grassed areas were treated with the now quite familiar method of teased-out carpet underlay and various scenic scatter materials. Trees and shrubs were made from twisted wire or rubberised horsehair with foliage mat and scatter sprinkled on. The colouring was studied very carefully from waste ground, embankments and various trees and hedgerows at the appropriate time of year, in this case autumn.

The study of colouring extended right through the construction. The buildings, made from DAS-covered ply, had their brickwork toned down, with roofs showing growth of moss and algae. Roads had dirty gutters and paths were bordered with vegetation.

Rolling-stock and operation

Locomotives and rolling-stock were being built specifically for this project, so Gordon had no qualms about weathering everything to suit this setting. To date three locos have been scratchbuilt, a 'C2X' Class 0-6-0, an 'E4' Class 0-6-2T and a 'K' Class 2-6-0, all LB&SCR classes that were regularly used in the Sussex area. The 'K' is not really suitable for such a small layout so only makes an occasional appearance, and Gordon freely admits that it was built purely because he liked them. Four other locos were made from kits, three Vulcan 'Terriers' and a Meteor 'P' Class 0-6-0. Two of the 'Terrier' tanks work regularly on the single-coach passenger trains, with the 'P' Class in reserve. The other 'Terrier' has been built as the colourful 'Brighton Works' shunter and, as with the 'K', is another piece of self-indulgence.

The sequence of operation is arranged for the four trains in the 'hands off' storage yard to be dispatched or received in such a way that at the end of a session the turntable is rotated to start the sequence again.

and any subsequent layouts. The theory was that this trestle could be assembled first and levelled before the layout proper was installed. This has worked well with this layout, but the disadvantage is that it produces a lot more timberwork to transport around and carry into and out of the various halls, some of which are not that close to unloading areas. Whether this universal trestle will ever carry the burden of other projects is still uncertain, but Gordon feels it was well worth trying out on this layout.

In the interests of reliability, and a slight doubt over his own ability to build decent track, Gordon used Peco products for the standard gauge permanent way. This has proved to be totally successful, with the slight exception of one turnout blade becoming detached on the first outing; a replacement was fitted and another pair made, and these have been carried as spares ever since - needless to say they have not been needed.

The track was all painted and the appropriate point rods and cranks fitted before ballasting. Much care was taken over the placement of the ballast, which is budgie grit, before it was secured with diluted PVA glue, tinted with water-based paint to tone down the ballast.

Scenery

The scenic levels were built up with various scrap materials, - card, crumpled paper, polystyrene packaging, etc - to fit the pre-cut contours on the baseboard sides and ends; these 'hard' edges helped to ensure that the baseboard joints were not too obvious.

Over the last five years Ditchling Green has been exhibited on many occasions, and consequently has travelled many hundreds of miles, most of them in its trailer and for much of the time being subjected to some of Britain's worst surfaces - the M42 takes some beating! Despite this, Gordon feels that the choice to keep the layout compact and transport it in a trailer was the right one for him. The thought that went into its design, to help protect it and ease its assembly, seems to have paid off, and a lot has been learned during this time.

Gas Street Yard
by Mike Hewitt

Gas Street Yard once again sets out to dispel the myth that to model in O gauge requires acres of space and a lot of capital investment. This layout measures 10 by 1 feet, a size dictated by the length of one wall of the owner's dining room, while the width was calculated to take up little of the living space, so that the room still retains its normal day-to-day domestic function almost unhindered (or very nearly). In addition, the layout was to be made portable so that it could be transported as easily as possible to exhibitions, and stored if domestic conditions necessitated it. Once the objectives for the layout had been determined, attention could be given to planning the layout in detail.

The planning stage is crucial to a small layout if it is to work successfully and maintain the operator's interest over a prolonged period of time. Many hours,

Gas Street Yard. Mike Hewitt

weeks and months of doodling on scraps of paper, measuring locos and wagons, juggling with points and deciding on scenic backdrops went into the preparation of the final plan - the temptation to jump in and get something running quickly must be resisted, otherwise disappointment will follow.

Baseboards and trackwork

The baseboards were constructed as two 5 by 1 feet units made up from 5 feet by 4½ inch lengths of 9 mm ply with 9 mm ply stretchers at 1 foot intervals to form a ladder-like structure. This was topped off with half-inch Sundeala fibreboard. The backscene and fiddle yard front were 4 mm ply supported on three-quarter-inch frame.

The problem of aligning facing baseboard joints was solved using 1 inch wooden dowelling fitting into 1 inch holes on the opposite board; rubbing the dowel with candle wax ensures a smooth fit. The baseboards are held together with two 10 mm nuts and bolts.

Folding legs were fitted to each baseboards unit, initially set to give a floor-to-track height of 3 feet. In practice this proved to be a little low for spectators, and has since been increased to 3 ft 9 in. Black material along the front and two sides screens the underlayout area and hides all the paraphernalia used at exhibitions. The fiddle/storage traverser holds six or seven wagons and a small loco, which is fine for general use.

For exhibition use, to create additional spectator interest and to prevent operators becoming bored, a greater number and variety of wagons are run, and this is accomplished very simply by using removable fiddle yards. In effect these are trackbeds with sides, removable ends and lifting handles, with a sec-

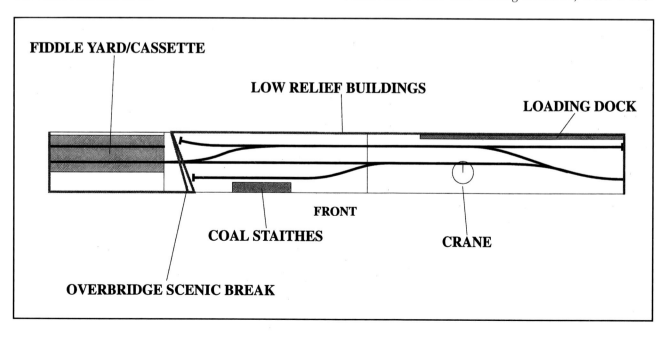

FIDDLE YARD/CASSETTE

LOW RELIEF BUILDINGS

LOADING DOCK

FRONT

COAL STAITHES

CRANE

OVERBRIDGE SCENIC BREAK

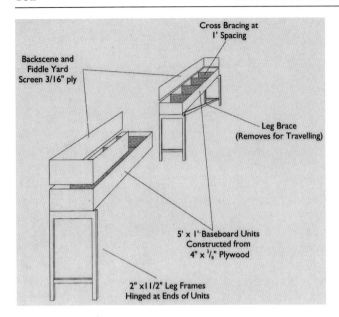

Gas Street Yard baseboard construction. *Mike Hewitt*

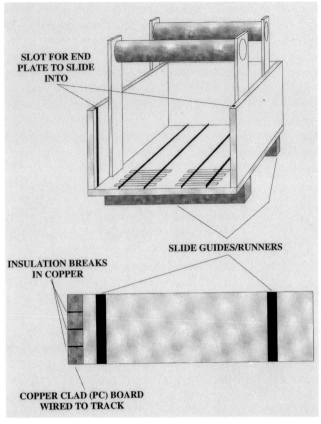

Diagrams of Mike Hewitt's fiddle/storage cassettes, showing (above) the end view and (below) the underside. (See also the photograph on page 28.) *Mike Hewitt*

ondary benefit of being used to store stock. In use, one of the fiddle/storage cassettes is put in place, the end removed and the stock shunted freely. When a change is required, the end is replaced, to stop stock escaping with disastrous consequences, the cassette is lifted out of position and replaced with another, the end removed, and operation continued with a different set of wagons. This idea is particulary useful for people who like to model different time periods or railway companies, as each storage cassette can store stock from a different era or company.

The track layout can make or break a small layout. The more time that is spent in the planning stages, the easier and more satisfying the layout will be. Gas Street Yard utilises five standard 6 foot turnouts, has three sidings that hold between one and four wagons, and a run-round facility with a headshunt capable of storing one wagon while still allowing a small loco to run round.

All trackwork is hand-made using Code 124 nickel silver track soldered to copper-clad sleepers. Points are changed electrically using Fulgarex slow action point motors with built-in change-over switches to change the polarity of the live frogs.

The track was ballasted using N gauge granite ballast laid in the normal way using a 50/50 mix of water and PVA adhesive.

Scenery

Two types of materials are used for the fabrication of buildings, Plasticard and foamboard/'kappaboard'. The latter is a laminate of fine foam between two outer layers of thin card; removal of one of the outer layers exposes the foam face, which can then be scored to represent brick, stonework and rendered surfaces.

The agricultural merchants at the extreme left of the layout is a proprietary resin cast product from BeeJay Models. All buildings are low relief (just the front wall) to save precious space in the operating area. A mess hut constructed from scored 1 mm ply fitted with lights, interior and additional details provides a point of interest at the right-hand end of the layout. Each building is painted a different shade or colour to create individuality, then weathered using thin colour washes and dry-brushing techniques.

The cobbled area is made of fine interior filler mixed with water/PVA solution, which helps to prevent cracking, chipping or splintering, the stone sets being scored into the surface. All other surface areas are laid with fine stone waste, again using a 50/50 water/PVA solution. This stone waste can be acquired from your local friendly stone mason, quarry, fireplace manufacturer or anywhere involved in the cutting of stone. Depending on the type of stone being cut, the waste can be obtained in various colours - Gas Street Yard uses a red shale colour.

A view down almost the entire length of the Gas Street Yard
layout showing how effective a long narrow layout can be.
Martin Hewitt

The platform/load banks are solid wood machined
to size, then covered in plastic for brickwork and
stone set surfaces, with individual platform edge flagstones made from card.

Electrical control

The general wiring is as simple as possible, both for
reliability and ease of fault-finding. Baseboards are
connected electrically
using a multi-pin plug
and socket, as is the
power controller to the
trackwork and points.
The controller, again
home-made, is built into
an old instrument case,

End and side views of the
baseboard/storage cassette
electrical joint arrangements.
Mike Hewitt

has a hinged lid that protects the switch-gear during
transit, and a schematic track layout incorporating
the point-operating switches in their relevant positions on the plan. The only drawback with this idea is
that on a unit intended to be used from both the front
(home use) and the rear (exhibition use), in one of
these positions the trackwork schematic is laterally
reversed. Loco control is effected through a simple
transistor controller, which provides good slow running.

Since the initial stages of completion of the layout,
working lighting has been installed in the yard, load-

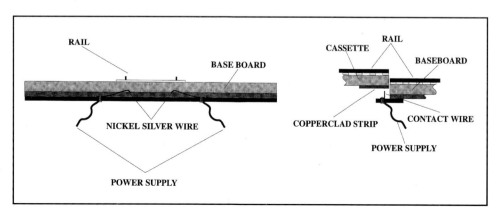

ing bay and mess hut area. Most of the wiring for this is self-adhesive copper tape used for the electrification of doll's houses. A separate power supply was built to power the lights rather than add an extra load to the loco controller unit.

Rolling-stock and operation

As the basic criterion was for a shunting layout, a small goods yard serving several industries direct was chosen to provide variety and interest. The variety of wagon stock can be enhanced by careful selection of the industries served by the yard. Typically food wholesalers allow for the running of open, closed, refrigerated and other specialised stock in both freight and passenger liveries. With this type of compact layout, where the number of vehicles on show at any one time is small, vehicle type and colour are used to attract and retain the spectators' attention.

Another benefit of using an industrial setting for a layout is that these types of buildings had a long lifespan. Gas Street can cover the period from the 1880s to the 1980s quite comfortably, and LNWR, LMS and BR stock and locos can be seen at work there. When planning a multi-period layout running into the later BR period, do not forget to take into account the longer wagon lengths that were used in the latter years.

All manner of materials and techniques were used in the construction of wagons operated on the layout - 1 mm ply, brass extrusion and Plasticard for scratchbuilt wagons, through to etched brass, white metal and injection-moulded plastic for kits. In the light of four years' running experience it has been found that wagons fitted with sprung buffers and axle compensation run with greater reliability, and all stock is fitted or about to be fitted with these modifications.

For obvious reasons the locomotives are either 0-4-0s or 0-6-0s. All are fitted with Mashima 1833 motors and 40:1 gears for slow running - of crucial importance for a shunting layout. Again the nondescript industrial setting allows the modeller to run not only locos from different companies/time periods, but also those rather quaint and attractive private industrial locos in their colourful liveries. Two LNWR, one LMS, two BR and two private industrials are on the Gas Street roster.

Operation of the layout is fairly simple. Gas Street Yard is attached to a larger yard/station complex the other side of the tunnel mouth/scenic break. Therefore, as all movements are within station limits, brake-vans are not required. Wagons are 'pulled' into the yard two or three at a time and distributed/exchanged round the various sidings utilising the run-

round facility. Wagons to be returned to the storage/fiddle yard are pushed off the layout.

Gas Street does not have its own self-contained exhibition lighting (yet) and difficulty was experienced in poorly lit venues with coupling three-link and screw couplings. To overcome this, experiments were carried out with auto-coupling systems. The Links system emerged as the preferred arrangement; it is simple to construct, install and operate, is unobtrusive and does not impede the use of the traditional three-link couplings should they be required. Initially only one set of stock was fitted with the auto-coupling system, but such has been its success and popularity with operators that all stock and locos will be retro-fitted.

A layout such as Gas Street has disadvantages as well as advantages; long trains and big locos/locos and tenders cannot be run, passenger stock is limited to a workers' train (one aging four-wheeled coach!), and there are no elegant curves, sweeping scenery, imposing structures, earthworks, etc. But if you consider it for a moment, there are not many people who can accommodate all these things indoors, or even outdoors, given the size of some modern gardens. However, as Mike points out, someone who wants an O gauge layout, does not have a great deal of space in which to put it, needs it to fit as unobtrusively as possible into a domestic environment and needs the investment to be moderate, should consider a small layout. The primary objective of Gas Street Yard was to prove the practicality of O gauge in a small space, and in this objective it has been successful.

Melbridge Dock
by Philip Parker

The trouble with building a layout for exhibitions is that you can build as big as you like and do not have to worry about doors and things, unlike a layout at home. However, for a small layout that has to go in the back of a Ford Fiesta for transport, its overall size is cast in stone (or steel?), and if it is to be used in a normal house, small has to be beautiful. In this case 'small' is two 3 by 2 feet baseboards plus a 3-foot fiddle yard.

Drawing a track plan from scratch, it is difficult to make it look realistic and have plenty of operating interest (sometimes the layout has to be operated for 8 hours at a stretch). In this case there was a simple solution - take one Great Western station plan, ignore the buildings and dimensions, add a siding and use that. From the plan it can be seen that the area where the dock is should have been the platform.

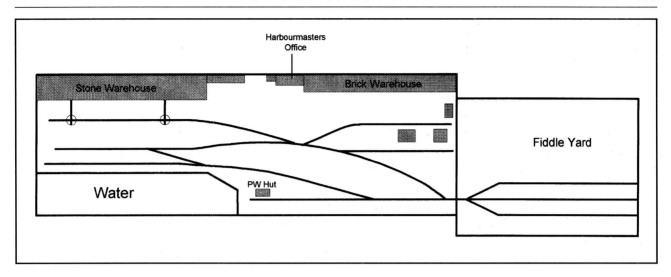

Melbridge Dock.

Baseboards and trackwork

The biggest advantage of belonging to a model railway club is that you are able to see what other people are doing. One of the members of Philip's club had built some baseboards out of plywood and, having carried them around a bit, this seemed to be the way to go. Philip adopted the same sort of design as would be used for chipboard/softwood boards - a top of 9 mm ply on a 6-inch-deep frame of 6 mm, with a cut out for the dock and the 9 mm backscene fixed to the top. To date the boards have not warped or twisted and the two scenic boards, when bolted together for storage, can be lifted by one person without major injury.

At home the layout is stored in an insulated box in the shed, or on top of the hot water tank. It can be set up in most rooms in around half an hour, to allow the 'testing' of a new locomotive for instance. Fortunately, its small size also allows it to be left up for reasonable periods of time to allow work on it to be interspersed with running sessions.

Whilst it is fun to operate at home, Melbridge was designed to work as an exhibition layout. In fact, the ability to run it at home has proved invaluable, with all those little gremlins being sorted out before the public are around.

Originally it all fitted in the back of the family

Fiesta, but an added display case meant that it needed something bigger, and this unfortunately meant the hire of an Escort van. After a while, however, it was noticed that it always seemed to look better at home than at a show. After a little thought it was concluded that the worktop over the water tank on which it was being built was 6 inches higher than then trestles, and this was making all the difference. To achieve this extra height would have been impossible with trestles (for they were not stable enough) so the 'Melbridge Leg System' was invented, as shown in the accompanying diagram. The new legs actually took up much less space than the trestles, so everything now fits in the back of a Ford Escort, which makes exhibition managers happier.

All track is SMP code 75 rail soldered to copper-clad sleepers. On a small layout a small rail section looks better, and with the limited track required it was not too arduous to build. More importantly, tight curves not available in proprietary ranges of point-

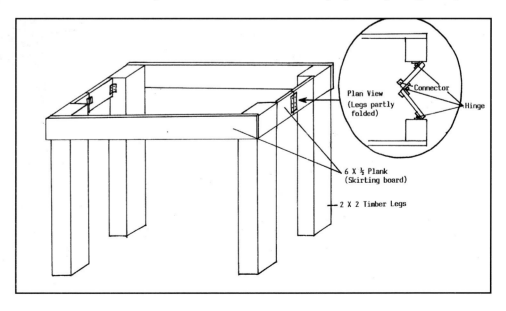

The 'Melbridge Leg System'.

work can be produced, allowing freedom in the planning stages.

Scenery

In a dockyard all the buildings are big. This may seem obvious, but how many layouts (in 4 mm) feature anything taller than 6 inches? Much research failed to provide warehouse plans, so a trip to Gloucester Dock museum with a camera and several books on docks was required. In the end rough card mock-ups were made to gauge sizes and shapes, and these were chopped around until they looked right. The finished buildings were then made out of Daler board, a high-quality thick card that is easily available from artists' suppliers. It cuts well with a scalpel and takes most kinds of glue. Once the shell was complete, Slaters Plasticard was stuck to it using UHU glue and PVA adhesive.

All that remained now was detailing. Acrylic paints were tried on the cobblestones, but it was found that the paint lifted at every attempt to weather them, so eventually enamel was used. In fact, the only use for acrylic was as a weak wash over the stone warehouse and on the backs of windows.

Philip Parker's Melbridge Dock layout. Note the short-wheelbase loco. *Tony Wright*

A novel aspect was the amount of talcum powder used as part of the painting process to flatten and unify the paint. It also gives the very slight texture that can sometimes be missing on Plasticard.

All the research paid off in the end, as many people claim to recognise buildings from the prototype, even if they are not quite the right ones (when showing in Southport, the brick warehouse was mistaken for Albert Dock). As mentioned earlier, tall buildings are unusual in 4 mm, especially on small layouts, and some people have questioned the scale. However, if you look at pictures of the prototype, see how the buildings dwarf the railway. One happy side effect of tall buildings is that there is very little backscene. What little is required is Peco townscene cut up into individual buildings and reassembled to give a different skyline.

In any photograph of a dockside from the 1930s onwards, the number of lorries is quite astounding, so any model has to have its fair share. These are either kits (Coopercraft or Airfix) or re-painted die-casts with the odd white metal kit thrown in. It is amazing what can be done with a die-cast lorry if you take it to pieces, strip the paint off and re-paint in matt colours (you do not see the shine on a real vehicle from a distance, so matt looks better on the model).

All dockyards also need a boat. In fact, there seem to be more and more boats on layouts these days. Unfortunately there are very few boat kits in 4 mm. What was needed was a small cargo boat, and it seemed only a Clyde 'puffer' would do! These boats plied their trade up and down the West Coast and did get down as far as Liverpool, and their relatively small capacity makes them an ideal candidate for the small quay. The BBC video of the early 'Para Handy' series, featuring the puffer *The Vital Spark*, supplied the inspiration, and a couple of books and a plan from the MAP plans service helped to produce a boat not exactly like any one 'puffer', but near enough to several.

The in-service alterations made to 'puffers' during their working lives meant someone building to an exact plan will be less accurate than one who employs a little modeller's licence. The whole thing was scratchbuilt in balsa and plywood, needing only a few selected accessories from the model boat suppliers to complete. As a finishing touch it was painted and weathered as *The Vital Spark*, with replicas of the crew from the TV series standing alongside.

Electrical control

The control panel is built into the back of the layout to save the necessity for lots of plugs and sockets. It is basically a track diagram with two push buttons for each point. The panel spans the two boards and the only connections are contained in a lead made up of four wires with a five-pin plug on each end. Layout wiring is *not* difficult, says Philip - it just looks it when you see a completed layout. In reality it is nothing more than a couple of simple circuits repeated many times. If you can wire up a light bulb, you can wire up a model railway layout. All the wires were stuck to the board with strips of paper and PVA glue, making them simple and easy to change if you need to get at a wire.

Rolling-stock and operation

For the dockside, only short-wheelbase steam and diesel shunters will do. Those in use at Melbridge Dock are a mix of modified proprietary models and kits. While the period is ostensibly late 1950s/early '60s, as long as the livery is right, modeller's licence has allowed several geriatric items to mingle with more up-to-date motive power. With slow running being the norm, wheel and track cleanliness is very important; regular use of a fibreglass pen and a Peco track rubber is therefore essential.

Most of the wagons are Parkside kits with the odd RTR or other make thrown in for good measure. All are fitted with Romford wheels; this, combined with a compatible track standard, allows for some very reli-

able running, especially bearing in mind the sharp curves in use. Couplings are Spratt & Winkle Mark 1s with either EM Gauge Society chain or droppers made out of staples. The chain does seem more reliable, and will gradually replace the staples, which have worked well, especially as the stock gets bumped around in transit. Permanent magnets are used for uncoupling with various markers to identify their location.

Both at home and at exhibitions, the layout is run on a free and easy basis with no timetable. In practice, most wagons have a notional 'home', eg banana vans to the stone warehouse (a fruit and wine importer), PW wagons to the front PW siding, pallet-based wagons to the siding near the fork-lift, etc. All this is based on trying to match wagon loads with the pile of the same load on the layout, although most of the wagons can go anywhere without looking out of place. Simply providing a mixed train in the fiddle yard sets up a shunting problem to keep an operator amused for an hour or so. Trains to the fiddle yard usually consist of wagons that seem to have been in view for too long.

All this allows interesting but relaxed operation. It is not usually appreciated by the casual attender of exhibitions just how long operators have to spend operating layouts during a show. At home most people will only operate for an hour or so, and can break for a meal without disappointing their public. The important thing is always to keep something moving. People have paid to see trains move and so that's what they should get.

It takes around an hour from turning up at a show to being fully ready for the public (track clean and all stock on), but this can be reduced. To improve the presentation a facia is included, but in order to fit it in the car and not take up too much space at home, both it and its supports had to fold in half.

Glastraeth, Sarn Helen and Caher Patrick
by Charles Insley

This is the story of three narrow gauge layouts that were built and exhibited between 1989 and 1995. All three are very different, but conform to three basic considerations.

Perhaps the most important consideration is that of space. This does not just mean that the layouts themselves are small, but that the space on them is used effectively. The largest layout, Glastraeth, measures 8 ft by 2 ft 3 in, while the smallest, Sarn Helen, measures 4 by 2 feet (Caher Patrick is 7 by 2 feet). Again, effective use of space does not mean cramming every inch of the layout with track - far from it. The main principle behind the use of space was that the layouts should be interesting to watch and to operate, while giving the impression of a railway in its environment.

The second consideration was that the layouts should be easily portable, while being able to withstand the knocks inevitable in being exhibited. These two may sound impossible to reconcile, but a compromise is possible. The layouts also had to be built by someone whose carpentry was extremely basic. In all three cases, the basic structure is a piece of flat board, usually plywood, braced by 'traditional' 2 by 1 inch timber. This may sound basic (which it is!), but it works.

Before assembly, any features below track level (rivers, harbours, low-lying land) were cut out of the main baseboard. Ironically, the heaviest layout is also the smallest; Sarn Helen, although only 4 by 2 feet, is a model of part of a slate quarry, and uses a lot of slate waste (genuine North Wales slate), which makes it very heavy.

The third consideration is to make the layout interesting and, as far as is possible, believable. The best layouts are not necessarily the most accurate ones, but the ones that make the person looking at it believe it really exists. This not only means making the track look as good as possible, but also the features beyond the lineside. In the case of Glastraeth and Caher Patrick, both of which are seaside termini, this has entailed creating a believable town around the railway.

On most narrow gauge railways the timetables were very sparse, and even on an exhibition layout there will be times when the train is not moving. The aim of all three layouts was to provide a suitable setting for the rolling-stock, and to create a setting that still held attention even when there were no trains. On all three this meant not only detailed buildings (usually built from Slaters or Wills embossed styrene sheet), but little scenes that attract the eye. On Glastraeth, for example, there is the policeman remonstrating with someone, while a dog does the inevitable on his bicycle, or the busy scene in the workshop, or the men repointing a chimney, or any number of such scenes. In terms of an exhibition layout, what goes on beyond the railway fence is equally as important as what goes on inside it.

Modelling narrow gauge brings many advantages, but also a few pitfalls. On the one hand the rolling-stock is smaller, and most narrow gauge railways ran quite short trains (although not all - one thinks of the Lynton & Barnstaple Railway in the 1930s, the County Donegal in the 1950s, or the Ffestiniog Railway today), which gives an advantage if space is a consideration. Narrow gauge also gives the modeller

the scope to do something 'different'. Even if a prototype is being modelled, all narrow gauge railways were very distinctive concerns, and if the modeller decides to go freelance, then the world is, as they say, his or her oyster.

The disadvantage is, of course, that there are no ready-to-run British outline narrow gauge models. Bemo and Lilliput make/made some delightful German and Austrian stock in HOm/HOe, but in 4 mm/1 ft and 7 mm/1 ft the British modeller has to rely on kits. This is, however, not the problem it seems. In 4 mm there are many injection-moulded plastic kits, which are very straightforward to construct, while a large proportion of the locomotive kits are made of white metal, and fit on ready-to-run 'N' gauge chassis. It is certainly possible to have a respectable fleet of engines and stock without too much effort.

All three layouts are freelance, in that they are not modelled on a particular railway or location. This does not mean that 'anything goes'. Another important part of railway modelling, and making a model believable (even if it is not modelled on a single 'real' location) is research. This can mean anything from going on field trips to your chosen area to reading books. The narrow gauge modeller is well served by some excellent books, which help to get the 'feel' of the railway right even if it is freelance. Real railways also provide an example of how to 'create' imaginary ones: Beyer Garratts might look a little out of place on a model based on the Corris or Talyllyn.

All three layouts are based on extensive reading of books, and the invention of a history or background to your own railway is as much fun as building it! The three layouts are also based on research in North Wales (in the case of Glastraeth and Sarn Helen) and Ireland (in the case of Caher Patrick). Many of the buildings on the layouts have been built from photographs taken on holiday; for example, the station building in Glastraeth is based on the old Ffestiniog station at Duffws in Blaenau Ffestiniog, while the chapel is based on that alongside the FR just to the north of Llyn Ystradau power station at Tan-y-Grisiau. On Caher Patrick the church is based on the 'Spanish Church' in Kilcar (Co Donegal), the main hotel/bar is based on the Harbour Bar in Killybegs (Co Donegal, and a fine place to be on a warm afternoon), while the cottages are based on ones from Connemara (Co Galway and Co Mayo), and the station is based on Achill station on the Midland & Great Western Railway (Co Mayo).

Glastraeth

This is the oldest layout, and was built in 1989-91. It is built to 'OO9 scale' (4 mm/1 ft) and, although free-

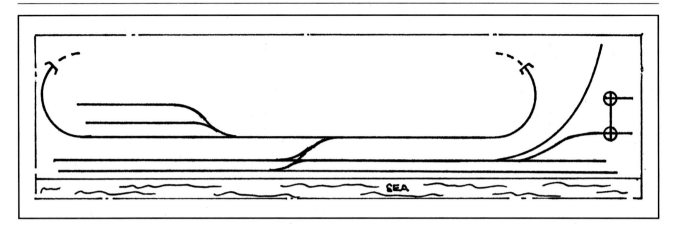

Top Glastraeth.

Above The coaster *Rachel Parry* docked at Glastraeth. Note the distinctly Ffestiniog ancestry of the loco and coach in the station. *Martin Hewitt*

lance, is based extensively on the Ffestiniog and Welsh Highland railways, and is set in the Ffestiniog area.

The track on this layout (and on all the layouts) is Peco streamline 009 track, which when weathered properly can look the part, and is an alternative to hand building your own. Electrics are kept simple, with one main loop and isolated sections in the station and yard. The points are operated by the 'wire in tube' method; the wire is also connected to a slide switch electrical contact, thus removing the need to rely on point blade contact.

The buildings are largely scratchbuilt, from a mixture of Slaters embossed plastic sheet and Wills 'Scenic Series' plastic sheets, and based on a variety of buildings in North Wales.

Sarn Helen

This layout was built in 1993, and is a model of a section of an imaginary slate quarry. Again, it is freelance, but is based heavily on pictures and drawings of the Dinorwic and Penrhyn quarries. The model is much compressed, as a compromise between space and the need to give the impression of height. The galleries of most slate quarries are staggeringly big, and obviously had to be reduced to fit on a small baseboard. The first level is roughly 30 cm above the base level, which gives a height, in model terms, of 75 feet, a fraction of what it would be in real life. Having said that, the model still creates an impression of great height.

The centrepiece of this layout is a working incline, powered by a cheap can motor and Meccano gears. Because of the layout's anticipated weight (it was always intended to use real slate on it), much of the upper level was built from 'foamboard', an artist's mounting board consisting of polystyrene sandwiched by cardboard, making it light and very strong - certainly strong enough to take the weight of track, engines and stock, and a considerable amount of scenery.

Again, the track is predominantly Peco (although Jouef small radius setrack is used on the spurs into the cutting sheds), and points operated by wire-in-tube as on Glastraeth.

Left Sarn Helen quarry.

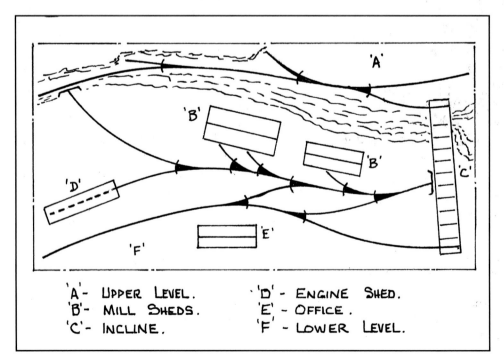

'A' - UPPER LEVEL.   'D' - ENGINE SHED.
'B' - MILL SHEDS.   'E' - OFFICE.
'C' - INCLINE.   'F' - LOWER LEVEL.

Above right The levels and electrically operated incline, Sarn Helen, showing how effectively the impression of height in conveyed. *Martin Hewitt*

Right The dressing sheds at Sarn Helen. *Martin Hewitt*

Caher Patrick

This layout is still under construction, and marks a departure from the other two in that it is built to a scale of 3 mm/1 ft on 9 mm track, giving a 'real' gauge of 3 feet, which is correct for Irish prototypes. Again it is freelance, but based heavily on the West Clare and the Cavan & Leitrim railways as they appeared in the late 1950s. Also, for the first time, models have been built of real locomotives and stock. Of all the layouts, this is the most heavily based on photographs (the fruit of two summer holidays), despite Ireland being further away and harder to get to than Wales!

Apart from the change in location and scale, the layout is built in the same tried and tested way as Glastraeth and Sarn Helen. However, each one has been more adventurous than the previous one; Sarn Helen incorporated an incline, and Caher Patrick has a motorised (Peco, inevitably) turntable, and illuminated buildings. Given that it is a harbour layout, the next thing to investigate would perhaps be real water, or a real fishing village aroma. Now that would be a challenge!

Left The view into the station at Caher Patrick, the scenic detail clearly emphasising its Irish setting. *Martin Hewitt*

Below The station and engine facilities, including the centrepiece motorised turntable, at Caher Patrick. *Martin Hewitt*

Helston
by Keith Gowen

Prototype modelling is not an easy job as you need a fair amount of information before you can even start to build the layout! Helston is such a project, and has been created in 3 mm/1 ft scale.

So how do you start to build a small layout that has to be transportable? The next few paragraphs give a brief resumé of how Keith Gowen undertook his project. First, collect as much information as you can. Keith collected many photographs and was assisted by information that appeared in one of the GWR station books published by OPC. This particular publication listed various magazine articles, and railway society stands at shows are also a very good source. One particular edition of the 1967 *Model Railway News*, written by Pat English, contained a track plan, which formed the basis of the layout.

This series of articles also contained drawings of the various buildings. Often the local Council can assist with site plans, and in Keith's case they did! Closer examination of one particular plan drawn to a scale of 40 feet to 1 inch established a natural 'L'-shaped layout that would finish at the Lower Trenneck Bridge. In modelling terms this meant that a pleasant scenic break could be achieved before the fiddle yard.

Consideration still had to be given to the actual size. Keith settled on a final configuration of three boards of 3 ft by 22 in with a curved section that would include a photographic display, making a 'flow-ing' curve; it was hoped that the display section would interest exhibition visitors. The complete layout measures 12 feet long by 4 feet deep, plus the fiddle yard section, which represents the remaining part of the branch, giving a total overall size of 12 by 8 feet.

Baseboards and trackwork

Once a good selection of information was gathered, construction of the actual layout could begin. Helston was always intended to be an exhibition layout to be transported in the average hatchback/estate car.

The baseboards were built using the conventional 2 by 1 inch timber frame carrying half-inch chipboard

Below Helston. *Courtesy* British Railway Modelling

Inset **A Post Office van awaits the arrival of the passenger train from Gwinear Road.** *Barry Norman*

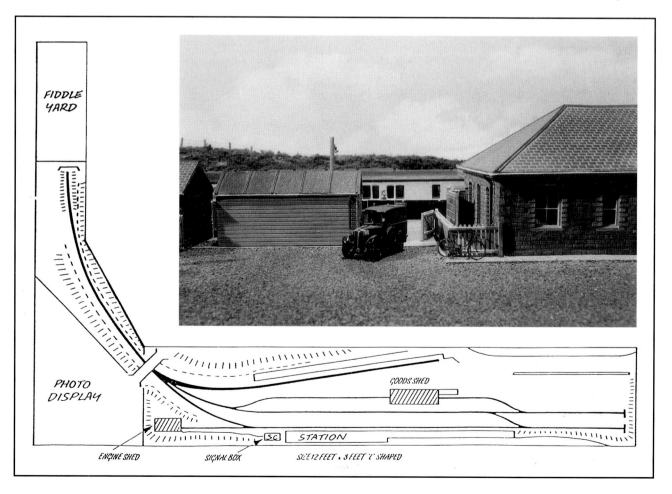

screwed and glued, which made a flat surface of 22 by 36 inches for each board. The layout is completely self-supporting, with one board being supported by two pairs of hinged legs that fold like those of a paste-table, the remaining boards being supported by one pair of hinged legs. The fact that all legs are hinged to the boards makes it very easy to transport and quick to set up.

The boards are aligned with carpenter's dowels, one of each pair resting on small support ledges, and are finally secured by quarter-inch coach bolts, making the whole layout very stable.

Once the baseboards were planned and constructed the trackbed was considered. Helston had a very interesting track plan, which included a siding that had to be accessed from the loading dock siding. This could have caused a few problems for the operator because room would have to be left in the loading dock so that vehicles could be reversed into the siding. The siding's purpose in life was for serpentine traffic being loaded via a shoot. Authentic help was at hand as it was discovered that this siding had been removed in the mid-1930s and not restored until the BR era; the layout could therefore be built in the period 1946-48, thus excluding the siding.

The trackbed is cork cut and shaped as required. All track was hand-built, constructed off the layout from code 80 rail on PCB sleepers by using the 3 mm Society track templates. A slight adjustment was made for the 36-inch radius curved point opposite the signal box, achieved using the Track Setta gauges. The other points were built to a standard 24- or 36-inch radius with a frog ratio of 1:6 or 1:7 as appropriate.

The track was sprayed with track colour, and once dry was glued to the trackbed with PVA glue and location pins. While wet, Scenic fine ballast was spread and the surplus brushed away for further use; adjustments were made to the ballast after 24 hours and the location pins removed. It is important to closely examine the track area in case any sections have been missed. All points are hand-operated using the 'wire-in-tube' method; the wire is attached to a small DPDT switch to change the polarity of the frog simultaneously with the point movement.

Scenery

Keith believes that if a model railway is to portray a picture, it must try to capture the atmosphere, particularly if it is based on a prototype. Here a good selection of photographs is a must, and Keith has possibly one of the largest collections of Helston gathered by one person.

The buildings were constructed from plans supplied by Pat English in the series of articles previously men-

tioned. They were all built from Plasticard utilising the full range of Slaters embossed sheet, particularly those specially produced for 3 mm.

When the layout was started there was no drawing available of the signal box and photographs were used to estimate the dimensions, checked against a ground plan for accuracy. Today there is a book on the branch published by Oakwood Press, which contains all the drawings and many photographs, including the signal box.

Once Keith was satisfied with the buildings they were painted, mixing various matt colours to obtain the right blend of stone, brick, etc. This can take many hours if the right texture is to be achieved; often the dry-brushing method was preferred. The blending or balance of colours was very important, but the end result has been well worth the time and effort, particularly when visitors to exhibitions express a great interest in the buildings because they remember the 'real' Helston.

Electrical control

There are few actual designated isolated sections because the points perform this function - power is only available to the 'road' set by the point.

The layout is controlled by a hand-held controller with power supplied by H&M controlled units. One of these units also supplies 16V AC to a circuit for the SEEP electro-magnets, which are installed in various parts of the layout for uncoupling rolling-stock. Due to restrictions 'under the scenery', centre-off spring switches supplied by SEEP are employed, which allow two magnets to be operated safely off one switch.

Operation

To achieve prototypical modelling the final aspect to investigate must be the operation of the actual branch line. As the period modelled is 1946-49, the best place to obtain railway operating details was the National Railway Museum at York. This was important as it provided Keith with a sequence to follow. This information is passed on to the exhibition visitor by the card system described earlier in the book, with details on one side of what is being undertaken on the layout, and operating instructions on the other.

The whole subject of railway operating is very interesting and more so when you are trying to operate a model of a prototype that closed over 30 years ago. When you are trying to achieve authenticity, people who worked in the environment can very often answer the problem you have spent many hours researching!

Exhibition layouts have to be entertaining, with smooth and reliable operation and working signals,

Components and assembly of the B&B coupling.

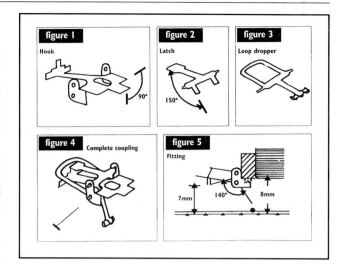

regrettably missing on many exhibition layouts today. Much has been written about Helston and Keith's attention to detail, which incorporates these points. The layout's successful performance is possibly achieved by the operation of the coupling system, and a large amount of research was undertaken to find the right one.

The B&B coupling system used is a delayed-action coupling that does not require you to stop over the magnet. Driving over the magnetic field de-couples the selected vehicle, which can then be pushed to the desired position. The coupling is worked by the magnet (hidden under the track) pulling down the tail, thus allowing the hook to rise. To be fully in control of the uncoupling, electro-magnets were used, being operated by a correctly rated 'push-button' switch or 'centre-off' sprung switch as previously mentioned. These couplings are available in 2, 4 and 7 mm, as well as 3 mm scale, and are reasonably priced. The assembly instructions are easy to follow and require no soldering; the components and assembly are shown in the accompanying diagram.

A Class '4575' 2-6-2T arrives at Helston while a '4545' shunts the yard prior to departure. *Barry Norman*

A general view of the station buildings after the departure of the early evening train to Gwinear Road. *Barry Norman*

Bayards Dock
by Bob Haskins

As with our other modellers, Bob believes that with any minimum-space layout it is very important to ensure that the track plan will not only fit the available space but also provide realistic operation and sustain the operator's interest for longer than half an hour. Keeping these high-minded principles to the fore, Bayards Dock occupies a space of 6 by 2 feet, operates correctly, has room for four or five complete trains and takes just over 3 hours to run through its timetable before all stock is back at its starting point.

Scenery

In a small space visual impact is important, which is why Bayards Dock needed three distinct and separate levels.

Modelling the dock at low tide provided the lowest of the levels, with the track being 2 inches above the mud banks. Running along near the end of the layout is a roadway and overbridge at a higher level, with low-relief buildings to further emphasise the level differentials. For example, from the bottom of the dock to the overbridge deck, the height differential is 4 inchs, and to the top of the warehouse it is 9 inches. The maximum depth of the viewed area is 18 inches, which, coupled with the different levels, helps to create the impression of a larger space than actually exists. Several people, seeing the layout for the first time, have thought it to be much longer than it is, so the theory must have been successfully translated into practice on this occasion! The front of the layout is framed and, apart from providing somewhere useful to hang the nameboard, it also directs the viewer's eye on to the model. The scene is lit by two 60 watt bulbs, care having been taken to get all the shadows pointing in the same direction.

Buildings suitable for the West of England

Left Bayards Dock.

Below The whole of Bayards Dock - all 6 feet of it - as seen through the viewing frame. The autocoach is arriving with the midday passenger service. *Ian Worthington, courtesy* Railway Modeller

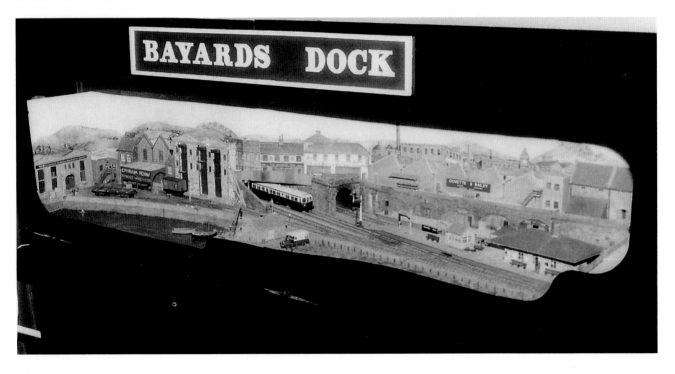

An '850' Class saddle tank departs light engine. Note the use of a mirror recessed behind the bridge to create the illusion of distance - the trick is to match the angle of the curve exactly. *Karl Crowther*

were selected so that a viewer would not find any architectural anomalies, such as Essex 'clapboarding' in what is supposed to be Devonshire. Some buildings were culled from drawings in the modelling press, while others were the result of measuring actual examples, either 'in the flesh' or from photographs. For example, the signal cabin is based on one that existed at Roach in Cornwall, Fry's tobacconists used to be in Plymouth, and the store hut in the foreground comes from Gara Bridge - all different locations but with a common, regional theme.

Small layouts are, in Bob's view, 'fun' - the opportunity is there to go to town on detailing such things as point rodding. Making two or three signals work is not too daunting a task, and the discipline of selecting appropriate locos and rolling-stock is no bad thing either.

Rolling-stock and operation

The fiddle yard at the rear of the layout is split electrically, thereby providing six storage areas for complete trains. All trains enter and leave the fiddle yard via a 2-foot-long sector plate, thereby saving valuable space. This sector plate also serves the bay platform, main platform and loop roads - it is, in every respect, the key to the whole layout. It dictates the maximum length of all trains; assuming 0-6-0T locos, there is

room for two short bogie coaches plus one van as tail traffic, or a goods train of four wagons and 'Toad' (brake-van). These train lengths allow for the occasional long-wheelbase wagon such as an 'Open C' or 'Mink C', but all bogie goods stock is banned!

The last 9 inches of each fiddle yard road is protected by diodes so that incoming trains can be safely driven to the end of the track without risk of running into the wall. When the controls are at the other end of the layout, this automatic protection has saved several mishaps.

All trains arriving in the station area do so on the main platform road. Goods trains stop with the loco adjacent to the signal cabin and water crane - apparently to get instructions from the signalman, but in reality to enable the loco to be uncoupled from its train.

The loco then runs forward under the bridge and reverses to shunt the goods yard, marshalling the departing train in the loop at the same time.

Quite deliberately, the distance between the point and the end of the line beneath the bridge restricts stock to an 0-6-0T and two 9-foot-wheelbase wagons. This means that incoming goods trains have to be split at the platform prior to shunting into the yard. An added complication is that the timetable requires an open wagon loaded with planks to be shunted into the bay road during each sequence, which means that the loco must run round the train, as the shunt is in the reverse direction from all those in the goods yard.

Some passenger trains and the parcels train also drop/collect horse-boxes or vans in the bay, and care needs to be exercised with timetable planning so as to avoid unnecessary shunting movements. In spite of appearances the prototype did, in practice, try to avoid such inefficiencies!

All the foregoing explains why a timetable is required, even on so small a layout. A sequential rather than a clock system is used, with every movement recorded on a numbered index card. These cards tell the operator the routes the train has to follow, which track in the fiddle yard to use and the control switch numbers of the points and signals to be pulled off. Since its first exhibition at Rochdale in February 1990, about six variations of the main timetable have been produced, each one reflecting slightly different traffic patterns and rolling-stock. Usually, relief operators have been able to follow the sequence without difficulty or developing too many grey hairs.

In common with most layouts, Bayards Dock now has too much rolling-stock and a surplus of locomotives. This does mean, however, that one can ring the changes from time to time. It is also possible to build up several different eras, such as 1950s BR or 1930s GWR, thereby adding even greater variety.

To run the normal timetable the layout needs 19 goods wagons, two 'Toads', three parcels vans or full brake-vans, two bogie coaches or an autocoach, plus five locomotives. To provide variety, all three 0-6-0T locomotives are different: a '77XX', '84XX' and an '850' saddle tank, with a Cambrian 2-4-0T and '14XX' completing the roster. Held in reserve are a '45XX' Prairie, a second '14XX' and a GWR railcar.

It is important to restrict goods stock to the type appropriate to the traffic the line would have generated. Therefore the majority of Bayards Dock's wagons are varieties of open vehicles and vans. Coal traffic, the main staple diet of the pre-war railways, is very light - the occasional 10T wagonload for the steam trawler or tramping coaster being the only requirement. While fascinating in their own right, 'Rectanks', bogie bolsters, Ocean Mail vans, etc, would not be required at such a place, and their appearance on the model would quickly destroy any illusion of reality.

The same policy needs to be followed with locomotive types, which is why small tank engines predominate - this type of location would not have been the haunt of 'Kings', 'Manors' or '28XXs'.

From its inception it took two years of not very plentiful spare time to build Bayards Dock, and it has since repaid that invested time by running without any major faults, both at home and at exhibitions as far apart as Livingstone and Bristol, plus quite a few others in between!

Bembridge
by Paul Mays

To find a prototype location suitable to model in a small space is not an easy task. If limited to a total length of 10 feet including the fiddle yard, it becomes almost impossible if you want to keep a little operating interest, without a little compromise. One way is to reduce lengths to three-quarter scale - if the prototype has a siding 100 feet in length, make it a scale 75 feet. This is a good way of bringing the length down without spoiling the effect.

If you only have 10 feet or so to work with, a through station with a fiddle yard at each end is out of the question, and the terminus-style station is the only feasibly option. But even a terminus station can be spacious, so if you want to keep to standard gauge a small example is necessary, and there was one in use on the Isle of Wight until 1953. With only three points and a short single platform, Bembridge is an ideal prototype for a small model railway layout.

To compensate for the lack of size and operation it is useful to include an unusual feature. Bembridge's main one, operationally, was the small turntable at the end of the platform. To call it a turntable is somewhat of a misnomer - a sector plate would be more appropriate because, although it was built as a turntable, it was only used to release the loco from the platform to the run-round road, barely more than a couple of feet. Originally only 16 ft 5 in in diameter, it was rebuilt in 1936 to accommodate the 'O2' Class 0-4-4Ts. Shortage of space was the reason for the turntable's existence, as there was insufficient room for the usual arrangement of turnout and headshunt.

With a curved platform of only 220 feet, or the equivalent of four 'Brighton bogies', reducing the length to three coach lengths and only running two still looks quite acceptable in model form. Opposite the platform, on the other side of the run-round loop, was a siding that saw little use in the last few decades of the line's existence. Originally for general merchandise, it ended its days being used for storage. Access to the siding was by a cart road off Station Road, which in itself was confusing as the station building was in the toll road later known as Harbour Strand, Station Road running along the other side of the railway land.

Another operational oddity was the rail-built chock used in place of a trap or catch point to prevent a wagon running away from the siding and coming to grief on the main line. This chock was positioned about 20 feet from the nose (or frog in model railway terminology) of the siding turnout. Pivoted on the outside end between two sleepers, it was about

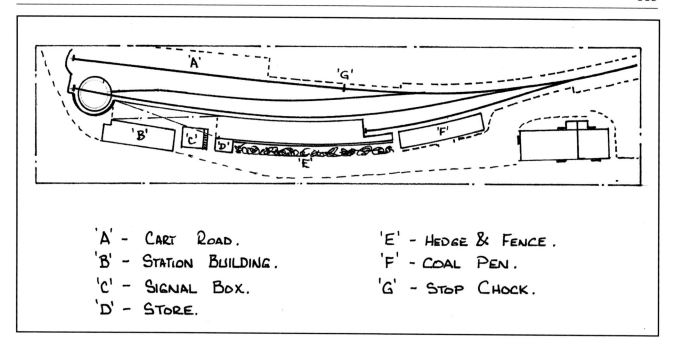

'A' - CART ROAD.
'B' - STATION BUILDING.
'C' - SIGNAL BOX.
'D' - STORE.

'E' - HEDGE & FENCE.
'F' - COAL PEN.
'G' - STOP CHOCK.

Bembridge - the layout.

2 feet long and rested in place against a stop when wagons were not being moved, the stop just being clear of any wheel backs.

The only other siding was the coal wharf siding, to the west of the station, just 120 feet long with the buffer stop at the end of the station platform. The siding served what the Southern Railway called a 'coal pen', which was in fact a set of five coal staithes with a corrugated iron roof - quite a grand facility for a small branch line. From a modelling point of view, operation into the coal siding is simple enough, as on the prototype wagons were more often than not propelled in from the next station, St Helens.

When the branch was built it seemed that no expense was spared; no wonder that the Chairman of the company responsible for the construction of the line, a certain Jabez Balfour, ended up in prison for debt. The station building was a grand affair, an elegant two-storey Victorian edifice with somewhat ornate brickwork. A signal box stood at the west end of the station building. The line was signalled in its early years, but because it was operated on the 'one engine in steam' principle, the Southern abolished all the signals soon after the Grouping. So Bembridge box was left with just four working levers, two for operating and two for locking each of the two points in the main line.

Next to the signal box, and separated by a footpath, stood a small store shed. Originally a grounded van body, it was replaced by a corrugated iron structure in the early 1930s. From the store for about 40 feet along the back of the platform there was a 4-foot-

high wooden fence, on top of which, about half-way long, there was a large station nameboard with notice boards at each end. From behind the nameboard to the end of the platform was a 10-foot-high hedge, trimmed regularly with vertical straight sides and a flat top.

Baseboards and trackwork

The layout is built on three 15 by 40 inch baseboards, which fit into a frame for transport to exhibitions. The baseboard frames are made from 2 by 1 inch timber with a surface of three-quarter-inch marine ply and half-inch fibreboard. The pivoted sector plate is half-inch plywood.

The track is Peco (code 75 rail) and the three points are electrically operated. The ballast is a mixture of sand and Cascomite, laid loose and sprayed with water. When dry it looks like the shingle ballast used on the Isle of Wight.

Scenery

Deciding what to include and what to leave out can be a problem when planning a model railway layout. If it is going to be a permanent layout, for your own enjoyment, then anything goes. But if it is planned to be a layout for exhibitions, a few details have to be taken into consideration. It has to be pleasing to the eye with an even look, or, as Iain Rice puts it, 'balanced'. With Bembridge this would depend on which side the layout was to be viewed. If from the seaward side, the buildings along Station Road could be included, but it would be unbalanced in as much as there would be too many at one end, unless the buildings set well back at the west end of Station Road

No 17 *Seaview* on the turntable at Bembridge, which was built to take Class 'O2' locomotives. As can be seen, it was a very tight fit! (See also the photograph on page 14.) Railway Modeller

Wight Railway, so its own 2-4-0Ts put in regular appearances, to be joined by the smaller 2-4-0Ts of the Isle of Wight Central Railway after the Grouping. As the 2-4-0Ts became fewer in number due to scrapping, 'Terrier' 0-6-0Ts became more common on the branch. As mentioned above, in 1936 the turntable was rebuilt to take the 'O2' Class 0-4-4Ts. During the work the branch was operated with a push-pull set and a 'Terrier'. When the turntable work was completed, all trains were 'O2'-hauled.

From the opening up to the push-pull stock, the coaching stock consisted of a wide variety of obsolete second-hand four- and eight-wheelers. The push-pull coaches were rebuilt LCDR six-wheelers converted to four-wheelers, and can be seen today on the Isle of Wight Steam Railway as Set 484. The remainder of the line's existence saw trains consisting of 'Brighton bogies' in sets of either two or three coaches.

The automatic couplings in the rolling-stock are Paul's own adaptation of the tension lock system using a 20 thou brass bar and a 15 thou steel hook. The hooks are actuated by magnets placed in the track.

The layout is not operated to any sort of timetable, and the stock used is influenced by a little modeller's licence! Otherwise it would be totally boring, as the prototype ran with one loco all week.

were included. The best way for balance is to have the layout viewed from the landward side, leaving out the Royal Spithead Hotel, as it was way too big, but including the house to the west end of the 'coal pen' along the toll road later known as Harbour Strand. This house is the building still standing at the time of writing, used as a store and workshop at the yacht club. The scenic break, where the trains go 'off stage', is hidden or disguised by trees. There were no structures blocking the view of the railway from Station Road, for there was just an open yard by the siding, and allotments beside the line almost to opposite the house mentioned above.

The station buildings were made of Plasticard and the scenery is mainly Woodland Scenics.

The turntable is 4 inches in diameter and is powered by a Portescap motor and gearbox. Two microswitches limit the travel because, as already mentioned, it is not really a turntable, more a sector plate. The decking is made from 1 inch styrene strip.

Electrical control

Wiring is simple and was kept to a minimum by having all three points and the control panel on the centre board.

Rolling-stock and operation

The first locos to work the branch on its completion in 1882 were a small Manning Wardle 0-6-0ST called *Bembridge*, with a 2-4-0WT named *St Helens* used as stand-by. In 1898 the line was taken over by the Isle of

Dallington Road
by Trevor Booth

Dallington Road was built in 1987 as an experiment. Having built several O gauge locos, Trevor had a feeling that a small 7 mm layout was possible with the sort of scenic and running quality associated with 4 mm scale but encapsulating the definite benefits of the larger bulk and sheer presence of 7 mm scale models. Being an experiment, the layout was never really intended for exhibition, or really to have a life beyond that of an inaugural test bed for O gauge.

Trevor felt that at the time, with very, very few exceptions, there was a scarcity of O gauge layouts of any size with halfway decent scenic work, let alone an authentic mix of scenic setting, structures, detailing and stock. In fact, while the sheer quality of engineering of locos, lever frames, signalling and, to a lesser extent, rolling-stock and individual buildings was often of the highest quality, the whole left a lot to be desired to his eyes, trained on 4 mm scale models.

It is all very well to be critical, but another thing to produce a model that satisfies these criticisms. A brief evolved for a layout that should

- be small, no larger than 10 ft 6 in by 2 ft
- be capable of some bucolic scenic work
- be as authentic as possible, ie no '14XX' pulling Caledonian coaches alongside diesels and Lima '4Fs'
- achieve an equality of overall standard and finish, not just rely on one or two items of excellence
- run well
- be capable of sustaining operating interest, despite small size
- create an overall picture.

The last point is the keystone to Trevor's modelling philosophy and attitude. Never mind the number of rivets - the thing has got to look right in totality. It's the overall impression that matters. This approach has been discussed in detail in Trevor's three books in 'The Silver Link Library of Railway Modelling' (see page 128), in which the detailed planning and building of a model railway is described.

Given that the layout was to be a test-bed for Trevor's attempt at 7 mm scale modelling, the brief he had given himself could ultimately be used to test the success or otherwise of the layout.

The layout also had to be different. A couple of visits to the Kent & East Sussex Railway provided the inspiration for Dallington Road - a might-have-been extension of the K&ESR to Dallington or, as with the Hawkhurst branch, a Colonel Stephens-engineered branch from

the Hastings main line to Dallington, the latter option giving greater opportunity for variety of locomotives. The name Dallington Road reflects the fact that, in true Stephens style, the station is some way from the hamlet it serves.

The choice of period posed the biggest problem - the obvious variety of locos and stock of the late K&ESR period, or the liking for the BR liveries, and in particular the lined black 'Terriers'? The latter won, and structure colours, some detail and the stock itself would be duly organised for the 1959/60ish period.

Planning a layout, working out what you can do and the frustration of realising that a 7 mm *Clan Line* won't fit your headshunt, even if you could afford the kit, is part of the fun, and a lot more pleasurable than building baseboards and trackwork, two aspects of the hobby that Trevor positively dreads! In any event, careful planning and preparation can save a lot of trouble and wasted expense later.

Baseboards and trackwork

The final track plan was evolved by Trevor's then 15-year-old son Andrew. The aforementioned dislike of building baseboards meant that, already having several baseboard frames to hand, salvaged from a previous EM layout, and each 3 ft 6 in by 2 ft, the layout would be built to a size that was a cumulative multiple of some of these baseboards.

Initially three were favoured, giving a total layout length of 10 ft 6 in, but by now the urge to compress was upon them (and there was a wall that was just big enough to give a clear 8 feet). Two baseboards were therefore used, giving a layout of 7 by 2 feet, but an overhanging sector plate gave a total size of 8 by 2 feet. A working layout could actually be made using this plan in the 7-foot length, but trains would be very short - one or two wagons or one small coach and a small engine, say a '14XX' or a 'Terrier'.

The baseboards themselves call for little comment,

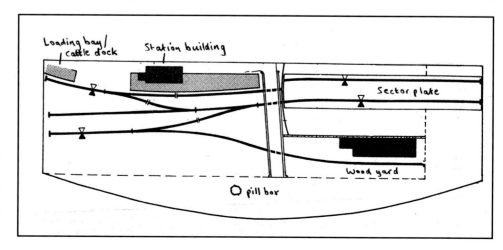

The final track plan of Dallington Road. The dotted lines represent the extent of the original baseboards.

being of the traditional 2 by 1 inch softwood frames and hinged legs, and surfaced with Sundeala board. Having been in use for some years on this and the previous layout, they have proved most satisfactory, despite protestations that softwood frames are less than ideal.

Having overcome one pet hate, baseboard construction, attention was now turned to the second, that of providing trackwork. The original intention was to use the excellent Waverley points kits and Peco plain track. However, there were attacks of conscience that said for such a small layout there really ought to be hand-built track, as detailed as possible with individual wooden sleepers and cast chairs; Slaters produce some very fine components for this type of track.

The thought of actually making track by this method appealed at an esoteric but not a practical level - far too time-consuming. Alan Gibson had not at that time brought out his track (now C&L), but a chance to visit to a second-hand shop to purchase a couple of Lima coaches also revealed 20 yards or so of Peco trackwork and four as-new points. The latter, offered at £1 each, solved the trackwork problem! The plain track is good from an appearance point of view if carefully laid and ballasted and the points give excellent running. There are one or two ideas for dealing with the over-scale gap between the running rail and the switch rail, which have yet to be put into practice.

Trevor considers the trackwork and ballasting to be just as important scenically as grass and trees. It must therefore take on an appearance that is commensurate with the overall effect being sought. In this case, deeply ballasted trackwork with clean, well-tended ballast was definitely not required, but rather an air of decrepitude and neglect. The track was laid directly on to the baseboard, pinned into place, then wired and thoroughly tested.

Although the plan had been worked out on paper, the actual position and shape of the track was finalised with the track on the baseboard. Here again this is a departure from the norm, because the shape and visual impression created by the position of the trackwork is, to Trevor, just as important as a correct and functional layout - back to the theme of creating an overall image.

The next stage was ballasting. Fine scale OO scale granite was poured over the trackwork and brushed into place. It also covered the area between the track and the yard to try to give the impression of the track being well settled in the station area. A mix of PVA glue and water was applied from a dropper to fix the ballast.

The whole lot was now painted with a dilute mix of rust and track colour applied by brush (Trevor has had an airbrush for several years, but can't get the hang of it!). While this was drying, Peco sleepers were applied to make the road access over the track near the cattle dock.

Now the fun began as the rails were painted a rust colour, as was each individual chair. The sleepers were also painted, one by one, with variations on a brown/grey mix in an attempt to give a faded, worn look. Black was added to the mix to represent grease on the sleepers near the tie bars. It took about four days for the glue to dry on the ballast, overnight for the track colour/rust to dry, about 9 hours to paint the rails, chairs and sleepers, and about 2 gallons of coffee to keep Trevor awake while doing it! It was, with hindsight, time well spent, but the next time it is reckoned that an even better result could be achieved in the light of experience.

Scenery

The station platform was made from Plasticard and represents the usual low type with a raised unloading area in front of the station building. The edging stones were cut from 20 thou Plasticard and added individually. The main surface is ash, and was represented on the model by using Woodland Scenics earth mix of a dark greeny-black hue, applied after the building had been added.

The cattle dock was of a similar construction with individual paving stones cut from 20 thou Plasticard. The dock was then painted and detailed, giving it a derelict air and overgrown appearance.

The station building was based on Northiam on the K&ESR and is a typical Colonel Stephens corrugated tin affair. A simple mock-up was made from cereal packets to give the idea of the finished model. Small though the building was, it looked rather too big at Dallington Road, particularly in width. The finished model was therefore reduced in width by some 25 mm and was visually better for it, although not strictly to scale.

The 'gents', such as it is, gave a rustic air to the model. Construction was of Plasticard using a 40 thou base covered in Slaters corrugated plastic; the roof was of the same material. The WD store in front of the sector plate was of the same material on 40 thou formers. The end formers were covered in brick Plasticard and a door was fixed on one end. The platform followed the same construction as the main one.

The road overbridge calls for little comment, being a rather crude affair of embossed plastic overlay on scrapwood formers, with bridge girders from Plasticard and microstrip. The excuse for this rather unlikely structure is that it was made to replace level crossings as part of the development associated with the build up to D Day, hence the WD store.

It must be said that there was not all that much scope for scenic development on the layout as it was. However, two semi-circular boards were bolted to the front of the basic baseboards giving an additional arc some 6 to 9 inches wide at its deepest point on which to develop further scenics.

The enjoyable bit was now about to start, after the drudgery of baseboards, trackwork and electrics. Resolved to move away from dyed sawdust and lichen, the search for suitable materials and methods began in earnest. The basic materials used were all available from BTA Hobbies. Their scenic scatters - the coarser ones being intended, it is believed, for smaller-scale foliage - were used for ground cover, differing colours and degrees of coarseness being mixed to achieve the desired effect. Rubberised horsehair from the same source was cut and dressed with the same scatter materials to provide the bramble and coarse undergrowth near the bridge and behind the buffers. Scale Link etched ferns and other undergrowth were also added; while they were quite effective, they were exceedingly difficult to 'plant' because of their fineness. 4 mm scale etches were used.

The post-and-wire fence was Websters GWR type, and Woodland Scenics coarse turf was used to represent vegetation at the base of the posts. Much time and effort was spent adding weeds and growth from dried grass and plants found during walks; these have survived surprisingly well and look effective, although probably now due for a replant. The climbing rose on the platform lamp was also made from dried plants.

The trees and bushes were from BTA and were quite effective. Those behind the cattle dock were from the deluxe deciduous range, ready made and quite inexpensive. The trees immediately in front were old Brittains birches with BTA foliage, while those on their own and in the foreground are made up from BTA etched tree kits; the bushes are from similar kits intended for N gauge trees!

Rudimentary point rodding was added from 1 mm square wire soldered to pins inserted in the baseboard and running to a lever frame near the platform end. This crude arrangement was replaced by more

This view from the road bridge shows the station and platform at Dallington Road to good effect. *Trevor Booth*

A simple picture, but very evocative of steam days on a branch line. It all looks so natural. *Trevor Booth*

sophisticated Scale Signal Supply components. Even a signal appeared!

Electrical control

The electrics call for little comment, and the track plan shows the arrangement of feeds. Control was by Compspeed Rambler, giving excellent control, although the hand-held unit was rather too fragile for comfort; the buttons tended to get pressed in and stick over a long operating session, causing some embarrassment when things stopped and the controller had to be opened up to rearrange the buttons! When you get the hang of it, pressing buttons for control is great, but from time to time you still expect to turn the knob and cause havoc when shunting!

Rolling-stock and operation

Locomotives and stock seem to attract a fair amount of attention, so some mention seems appropriate. Two locomotives were usually used, both appropriate to the K&ESR: an ex-SECR 'O1' Class 0-6-0 built from Jidenco and a Vulcan 'Terrier' 0-6-0T.

On a layout of this nature the locos have to run well and reliably, and, barring operator error, 95 per cent of the time they perform faultlessly. The 5 per cent is usually due to dirt on the wheels or a plunger pick-up that has stuck. The large type of plunger pick-ups are excellent, but there is less conviction about the finer type, which have been found, with a bit of use, to wear a groove in the housing and then fail to function properly. Those on the 'Terrier' were of this latter type, and the first set were replaced after six months use because of this.

The key to good running, Trevor believes, is nothing more sophisticated than a good pick-up and good concentric gears. Both locos had Mashima 1833 motors and 40:1 gears from Ultrascale; no fancy gearboxes, cradles or the like were used, but it was often assumed that RG7s were installed. Rather expensive! The locos and stock were not treated specially, but were merely part of the whole and as such had to be compatible in all respects, including standards of detail and finish, with the rest of the layout; they were not intended to be static museum models.

As far as can be recalled, goods stock at this period was by and large dirty and battered. Alas, Trevor finds that this is rarely reflected in the models seen; he certainly cannot recall trains of clean grey mineral wagons! The goods stock was therefore finished to reflect his recollection of their appearance *circa* 1959/60 and was well weathered, with just the odd clean(ish) item. Every wagon was weathered to some degree - even the clean-looking brake-van. He received a rebuke for showing limewash stains on the cattle wagon; limewash, he was told, had long ceased to be used by the

period of the model. You live and learn - it's all part of the fun of exhibiting!

There was initially a shortage of vans, but one or two varieties were constructed to remedy this, and the Sprat & Winkle ex-LSWR horse-box - used now for strawberry traffic - was added to the stock.

Coaching stock was somewhat limited: an ex-SECR 'Birdcage' brake from a DJB kit and an ex-LSWR van from a Highfield kit, the construction of which was detailed in MRC in 1987.

For a layout of this nature there is an argument in favour of automatic coupling as opposed to the big hand from the sky and overscale 'shunting pole'. However, experience of automatic coupling on EM layouts and, to a lesser extent, what Trevor has seen in 7 mm scale, suggests to him that so far a system that satisfies him from an appearance point of view with total reliability does not exist. He was therefore initially happy with screw and three-link couplings - it is just the oversize hand that is the problem.

As a first attempt at O gauge, Trevor was reasonably happy with the end result. It could be bettered, and the lessons learned in its building and exhibiting were noted for subsequent layouts. Exhibiting is an enjoyable aspect of the hobby, and Trevor was astonished at the interest shown in the layout and at the number of exhibition invitations it received. Considering that Dallington Road had not been designed for this purpose, it seemed rather strange!

Let Trevor now conclude with the answers to some of the most common questions he was asked, in the hope that the answers may encourage more O gauge modelling:

- The current crop of locomotive kits from Vulcan, Springside, DJB, Slaters and others are straightforward to build and, given time and a little patience, are well within the capabilities of most modellers - Dallington Road's 'Terrier' was built by Trevor's then 14-year-old son with virtually no help from his father.
- The locos were not fully compensated but performed equally well. The 'Terrier' used the designed-in Flexichas principle, whereas the 'O1' had a rigid chassis. Both had the same motor and gear types and plunger pick-ups.
- Most of the transfers used on the locos and stock were intended for 4 mm scale!
- Except for the fencing posts and embossed Plasticard, all other materials - including signs, posters, trees, etc - were also intended for 4 mm scale or smaller layouts.
- It is actually much easier to model in 7 mm scale than 4 mm because the bits and pieces are that much easier to handle. The biggest problem is

knowing when you are beaten and not carrying detail too far!

- The techniques and materials used were no different from those in 4 mm scale, but obviously sheet materials might be thicker and support for structures more important.
- There is a vast and growing range of 7 mm kits and other items. Forget the old crude models and kits at exorbitant prices - they are still around, but the new generation of models and components are of a quality of design that surpasses even the better 4 mm scale kits.
- The Gauge 0 Guild has been synonymous with the recent development of O gauge and its popularity, and is of necessity a broad church of people modelling in 7 mm scale in all its variants from Hornby clockwork to Scale Seven.

Dallington Road was sold in 1990. However, there is the distinct possibility that it may be rebuilt in the near future, but perhaps not as a KESR prototype!

Brookhurst Stabling Point
by Justin Adams

Finally, we return to a 'home-grown' model. This small layout is now 13 years old and was built by Justin when he was 13. It measures 5 ft 6 in by 1 ft 4 in and depicts a diesel stabling point. It is totally self-contained and rests on two trestles.

Baseboards and trackwork
The baseboard was made in the usual way from 2 by 1 inch timber with a surface of MDF (medium-density fibreboard).

The trackwork is all Peco, using four left-hand points and one right-hand point. They are all operated by welding rod, one end of which fits into the hole in the middle of the tiebar and the other protrudes through the baseboard frame at the rear and is then turned at a right angle to provide a vertical handle over which is fitted a piece of quarter-inch-square timber for easy pushing and pulling.

The track was covered as before with a mixture of Polyfilla mixed with black powder paint, which was trowelled on using a knife and forefinger.

Scenery
The main scenic feature - which hides the hidden sidings - is a low-relief factory built from a Heljan brewery kit, and is very effective. Justin first painted it with Humbrol brick red, then later weathered it by painting over it in sections with matt black wiped off with kitchen roll while still wet.

Justin likes adding detail to his layouts. There is a single working colour light signal with two workmen attending to a fault, the refuelling depot, the yard lights, the grounded coach, the small hut, the bike shed and the various bits of clutter and little cameos that all bring a small layout to life.

Electrical control
Prior to ballasting, the layout was fully wired and the switch panel situated on the extreme right-hand corner at the rear of the layout. This is a very sturdy and compact old bomb-aimer's switch panel that Justin picked up at an exhibition cheaply some 16-17 years ago. The wiring is simple, as the layout only requires two feeds and the rest are dead sections so that a number of locos can be stored on the various tracks.

Rolling-stock and operation
Essentially the locos move in and out of the yard and there is a daily run with oil tankers to fill up the small underground storage tank, which is presumed to be next to the refuelling point.

Justin runs a variety of locos on the layout, includ-

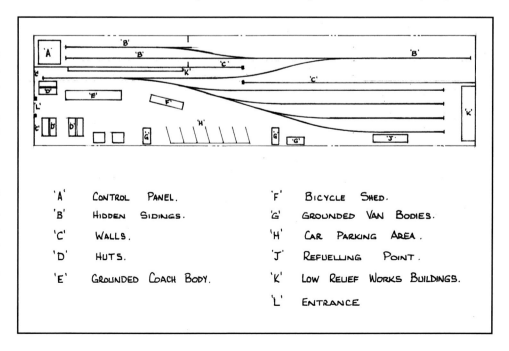

'A' CONTROL PANEL.   'F' BICYCLE SHED.
'B' HIDDEN SIDINGS.   'G' GROUNDED VAN BODIES.
'C' WALLS.   'H' CAR PARKING AREA.
'D' HUTS.   'J' REFUELLING POINT.
'E' GROUNDED COACH BODY.   'K' LOW RELIEF WORKS BUILDINGS.
                               'L' ENTRANCE

Brookhurst Stabling Point.

Left One end of Justin's Brookhurst Stabling Point layout. The wide view shows the amount of detail one can pack into a model without it becoming overpowering. In fact, far from being overpowering, I believe it is a positive asset on a small layout. *Barry Poultney*

Below left A close-up view of the refuelling point with a variety of diesels standing on the sidings. *Barry Poultney*

Class 03s and 08s can be seen, and at the other end Class 45s and 37s.

At exhibitions the layout is operated to a sequence timetable, which is always very satisfying. It is also interesting to see people's reactions to the list of scenic detail items displayed - they seem to treat it as a challenge to find them all!

As can be imagined, this is a very easy layout to take to a show. The layout itself, two trestles, one stock box, and two plastic stacking boxes easily fit in the car, and the whole thing is quickly erected and dismantled. On one celebrated occasion, all except the trestles were fitted into Justin's Mini! A friend bought the trestles home a few days later. Had the layout incorporated folding legs, the whole thing could have been carried in the Mini. Who says an interesting and satisfying layout can't be accommodated in a small space?

ing a Class 26 and 27, both of which were converted from Lima Class 33s when he was a teenager. The beauty of a layout such as this is that you can legitimately run large and small locos on it without them looking out of place. Hence at one end of the scale

INDEX

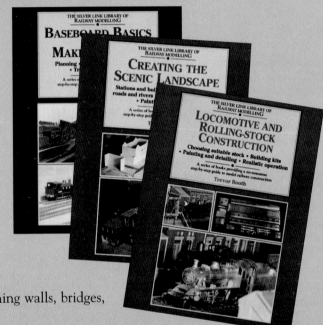